Pr

One Woman's Camino

This engaging narrative is not simply a mother-daughter story set on Camino de Santiago; it goes deep to reveal how that sometimes-complicated relationship can lead to transformation and mid-life self-discovery. *One Woman's Camino* is an insightful, true story about a modern, corporate woman overcoming obstacles on the ancient pilgrimage route.

Stacey Wittig, author of
Spiritual and Walking Guide: León to Santiago

By page 10 of *One Woman's Camino*, I felt I needed to grab a Rand McNally and set out on an expedition of my own. When a story immerses you in the emotions, the struggles, the discoveries, and the physical energy of the author, it's truly compelling for the reader. The biggest gift for me is that it's not enough to live vicariously through Tracy's trek—I am inspired to take my first steps on a new expedition!

Ann Deeter Gallaher, co-author
Women in High Gear and *Students in High Gear*

If you have ever wondered why people walk the Camino de Santiago, or if you have considered undertaking the pilgrimage, you will enjoy reading *One Woman's Camino*. Author Tracy Pawelski weaves together insights about travel, spirituality, and self-awareness as she takes readers on her 500-mile journey. With an engaging sense of reflection, she writes honestly about sharing the trip with her daughter, the camaraderie of other pilgrims, and the necessity of spending time alone. *One Woman's Camino* prompts a new-found appreciation for the pathways of life.

Nancy McKinley, Ph.D.,
Professor, Wilkes University
Graduate Program in Creative Writing

One Woman's Camino is a delightful read describing a dear friend's adventure trekking Spain's El Camino de Santiago. This book tells the story of a career executive who steps back from the spotlight of a fast-paced and high-powered career to trek 500 miles on the ancient pilgrimage. Tracy opens her soul with each step and ruminates on her failings, ambitions, habits and successes, while beginning to seek her own way. Each chapter follows the threads of her own revitalization, and I felt myself yearning to be brave enough to tackle my own Camino!

Diann Roffe,
Olympic Gold and Silver Medalist, Alpine Skiing

A generous and delicious helping of food for thought. A book you will remember.

Don Sarvey,
co-author of *Pioneers of Cable Television*
and author of *Day of Rage*

Take the journey of a lifetime as you travel alongside this fiercely independent and successful woman. Tracy unpacks all of her baggage; from the physical aspects of making such a trek, to the interaction between a mother and her daughter, to the search for reconnecting with her faith. Tracy's experience drew the world closer together for her. Let it do the same for you!

Tracey C. Jones,
Leadership Author and Expert,
Tremendous Leadership

ONE WOMAN'S CAMINO

Each Step the Promise of a New Beginning

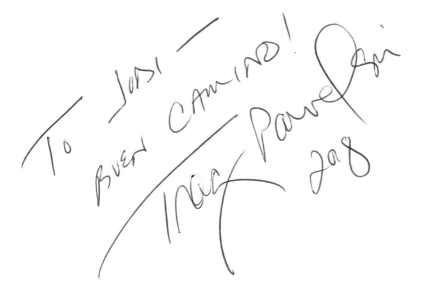

Tracy Pawelski

ONE WOMAN'S CAMINO
EACH STEP THE PROMISE OF A NEW BEGINNING

Copyright © 2018 by Tracy Pawelski

All rights reserved. No part of this publication may be reproduced, distributed, or transmitted in any form or by any means, including photocopying, recording, or other electronic or mechanical methods, without the prior written permission of the author, except in the case of brief quotations embodied in critical reviews and certain other noncommercial uses permitted by copyright law. For permission requests contact the author.

To contact Tracy:

  Website .... www.tracypawelski.com

  LinkedIn .... www.linkedin.com/in/tracypawelski

The poem "Finisterre" by David Whyte from his book *Pilgrim* is printed with permission from Many Rivers Press, www.DavidWhyte.com, copyright © Many Rivers Press, Langley, WA USA.

To contact the publisher, inCredible Messages Press, visit www.inCredibleMessages.com.

Printed in the United States of America

ISBN 978-1-7322510-0-7 ... paperback

ISBN 978-1-7322510-1-4 ... eBook

Book Strategist & Editor ..... Bonnie Budzowski

Cover Design .... Bobbie Fox Fratangelo

Cover Photo .... Caroline Combé

Dedication

With love and gratitude to Rick, Juliet, and Danny.

You are the pixie dust in my world.

RICK, JULIET, TRACY, AND DANNY

Acknowledgments

One Woman's Camino is my first book. And it didn't start as a book; it began as a daily travel blog from Spain. Thank you to all of the folks—family, friends, neighbors, colleagues and even strangers—who took the journey with me from the comfort of their kitchens and back porches and gave me the encouragement to keep writing and speaking about my experiences.

Thank you to the open-hearted Camino community, a community that epitomizes the spirit of fellowship and faith. Special thanks to my personal Camino angel, Camille Baughman, whose gentle guidance I continue to seek.

To all of my Camino companions, but especially to Caroline Combé from Amsterdam and Chuck Richardson from Belfast who have had a lasting impact on my life beyond the stretch of time we shared on the trail. I hope this story brings back fond memories and makes you smile.

Thank you for the generous time and priceless counsel of friends and fellow authors—my writing crush, Dr. Nancy McKinley, Professor of Creative Writing at Wilkes College; author and leadership guru Tracey Jones; and fellow travel writer and Camino doyen, Stacey Wittig.

Thank you to my book strategist and editor, Bonnie Budzowski at inCredible Messages, who coached a new author with an experienced and deft hand.

I am blessed to have smart and loyal female friends in my world, women without angles and hard edges who have cheered me on, including Lauren Burns, Johanna Grosgurin, Charlotte Kenyon, Pam MacKinnon, Arlene Putterman, Ginny Roth, Kim Schaller, Debbie Smith, and Laura Williams. Thank you for your love and laughter!

To my parents, Rose Marie and Dale Updegraff, who have always believed in me, loved me for who I am, and supported my decisions to go big or go home. I am who I am because of you.

To my children, Juliet and Danny, you bring me so much joy!

Juliet, I hope this book captures an unforgettable, once-in-a-lifetime chapter in our own story as mother and daughter. Thank you for saying yes. Keep writing and dreaming big.

Danny, keep leading with your smile and be careful skiing the trees.

I am so proud of both of you and love your sense of adventure.

And to my husband, Rick, my biggest fan and RFL. Thank you for picking me. How lucky am I.

CAMINO DE SANTIAGO

CAMINO FRANCÉS

SANTIAGO DE
COMPOSTELA
SARRIA
LEON
ST. JEAN
FINISTERRE
BURGOS
LOGRONO
PAMPLONA

France

★
MADRID

Portugal

Spain

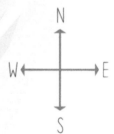

CONTENTS

———— Chapter 1 ————

COURAGE

A journey of a thousand miles begins with a single step.

~ Lao Tzu

When people learn that I walked 500 miles as a pilgrim on El Camino de Santiago, they often ask, "How do you walk 500 miles?"

"One step at a time," I reply.

Walking one step at a time on El Camino is a good metaphor for life and the central theme of this book.

This 1000-year-old pilgrimage across northern Spain continues to capture the hearts of modern-day seekers. On the most common route, the Camino Francés, a steady stream of pilgrims sets out each year from St. Jean Pied-de-Port in the French Pyrenees. They follow ancient footsteps into the stormy

Basque country and onto the unforgiving Meseta, Spain's high arid plains. Finally, they reach the northwestern corner of Spain as they walk through green and lush Galicia and into the ancient city of Santiago de Compostela. Here is where believers say the remains of St. James are buried.

What is everyone searching for on Camino?

People walk El Camino for any number of reasons, and each of them has his or her own story sprinkled with the pixie dust that Camino kicks up. My personal trek on El Camino de Santiago began as a mother-daughter journey across Spain. Along the way, however, it became a 35-day pilgrimage of personal reflection. In no time at all, it became clear that this was *my* Camino, a journey of profoundly personal insights and growth. Ask anyone who has walked Camino; it has a way of teasing out life's most meaningful lessons of trust, community, gratitude, and forgiveness. Camino has a way of offering an opportunity for reflection and spiritual sustenance in today's world of distractions.

This book chronicles one woman's Camino and how the journey served as an unmistakable metaphor for the values we all share—ways of living and behaving that can become buried as a result of busy, workaday lives. I want to share my story because we are all looking for an inspired next step in this journey we call life. Many of us are looking for the encouragement to begin.

You'll find that the following chapters are organized around such timeless themes as simplicity, resilience, encouragement, and faith. The last chapter is about the reward of completing the Santiago pilgrimage. But you only get to reap the rewards of any journey if you are willing to put one foot in front of the other and take the next step.

Here's the thing about taking the next step. You can't see too far down the road. In fact, most of us can only see the next step. And, frankly, life is so much more interesting that way. Maybe one day we'll be able to see the future, but I'm not sure it will make us feel any better. What fun would it be to know exactly what's ahead?

But it takes courage to begin. It's easy to become paralyzed about making the wrong decision. On their road to adulthood, my kids—Juliet and Danny—were sometimes overwhelmed with which way to turn, afraid that they might misstep. "It's not the rest of your life," I would tell them. "It's just the next step." All any of us can do is point ourselves in the direction we want to go and get moving.

When you focus on only the next step and know that it's not a permanent state of affairs, that step becomes less intimidating. If you don't like the results, begin again!

Walking El Camino de Santiago was an opportunity for me to take my own advice and put one foot in front of the other in the direction I wanted to go.

This mother-daughter journey wasn't always easy, and Juliet and I didn't always walk together, but it was one of the most rewarding expeditions of my life. For me, it was a once-in-a-lifetime break from a stressful career and a chance to deepen my relationship with my daughter, who was in transition between childhood and womanhood. The gifts I received from the journey, however, extend far beyond the satisfaction of walking into Santiago after 35 days. The space to reflect without distraction and the spiritual food I received along the way helped me to course-correct to my deepest values, personal priorities, and universal truths. And walking El Camino de Santiago with Juliet gave me my next inspired step, something I sorely needed.

Once I said out loud that I was going, I was committed. All in. No turning back. I kept asking myself, "What am I so afraid of?"

Into the Unknown in the Pyrenees

Chapter 2

REINVENTION

*This beginning has been quietly forming, and
waiting until you were ready to emerge.*

~ John O'Donohue, *For a Beginning*

For 21-year-old Juliet, wanting to walk Camino
and return to a part of the world she once called
home wasn't a big stretch. When Juliet turned 17,
she left for Spain as a Rotary International exchange
student. She spent her high school senior year in
Baiona, a lovely port city in the same northwestern
corner of Spain as Santiago de Compostela.

Baiona sits on the Atlantic coast just north of
Portugal. An impressive 16th-century walled castle
juts into the sea and can be circumnavigated for
stunning views of the Atlantic and the steep hills
above the town. Wild horses roam those hills.

When news of the New World reached Spain, it
reached Baiona first. A little off course, Columbus's

Pinta landed there on its return trip in 1493. Today a replica of the Pinta is tethered to a dock in Baiona's harbor and, for two euros, you can board and tour it.

Modern-day Baiona is a tourist town rich in history, coastal beaches, and local seafood. Hungry for Galician octopus and a rare gooseneck barnacle called percebes? Baiona is your place.

For someone who loves the ocean with all her heart, Juliet's destination could not have been a more perfect fit.

When Juliet returned to us in the States, she was fully fluent in Spanish and had a new kind of confidence from her year abroad. We were not greatly surprised when she announced after college that she planned to return to Spain, walk Camino, and put her Spanish into practice. She loved to speak the language and still had her charming Galician lisp. Juliet didn't have any concrete job prospects upon graduation, but she did have her next step.

So how did Juliet's decision to walk Camino become my next step too? How did I get from the hallways of Corporate America onto the byways of rural Spain?

Well, the first thing I did was ask Juliet, "Can I join you?" I didn't know until later that Rick had let Juliet know that I was interested in walking Camino too. Juliet will tell you that she didn't know what to think at the time about how my involvement would change the nature of *her* trip. She had a few days to adjust to the notion before we sat at the kitchen table and I gently inquired if I could come along.

By saying yes, Juliet gave me the permission I needed to take the next inspired step in my own life's journey. I still find it a bit remarkable that she said yes. After all, what 21-year-old wants to walk 500 miles with her mom? Kudos to Juliet for having the grace to let me join her.

But why did I need Camino?

I had reached a point in my career where I was hungry for a new beginning and had been looking for an exit plan from my current job. After a lot of soul-searching and planning with my husband, Rick, we made the decision together that it was time for me to move on to something new. Rick had always supported my willingness to shake up the status quo, understanding that the safest place is not always the best place.

At age 51, I was feeling stuck and increasingly desperate for a change. I had spent a decade handling U.S. communications for an international grocery store chain and led teams responsible for media relations, crisis communications, and consumer affairs. I managed a foundation dedicated to fighting hunger and helping kids. I spent ten joyful years in the company and loved the grocery business: the fast pace, my colleagues' work ethic, and the hands-on nature of retail.

But a job that might look like I had it all was eating me up. It was time to move on and create something new, even if I didn't know exactly what. I decided that Camino would give me my next step and a chance to reflect on what I wanted to do when I returned from Spain. I hoped that I would be able to make a meaningful contribution in another way, even though I didn't know how. Like walking across a bridge and into the fog on the other side, I had to trust that the shape of things would come into view.

If you are contemplating your next step, don't let fear paralyze you. But also understand that the road to reinvention takes courage. At the same time, rest assured that reinvention does not require you to leave your job, fling yourself across the world, or even walk Camino. But for me, the road did require that I disrupt my comfort zone and begin moving in a new direction.

As I looked out on the horizon of my life and thought about joining Juliet on Camino, my next step crystalized. Here was something I could get excited about. I could throw myself into planning for a step that I could now see.

I also was enthralled with an opportunity that I figured I wouldn't have again, an opportunity to go on an adventure with my daughter, whom I loved dearly but didn't always understand. Camino offered a chance to find common ground with Juliet and carve time out of my busy life for personal reflection and introspection. I understood that I was in the sweet spot. I had the resources, my health, and now the time to do what I wanted to do. I kept thinking, "If not now, then when?"

Trading in My
High Heels for Hiking Boots

Chapter 3

FAITH

*Truly I tell you, if you have faith as small as
a mustard seed, you can say to this mountain,
"Move from here to there," and it will move.
Nothing will be impossible for you.*

~ Matthew 17:20

El Camino de Santiago has been calling to pilgrims for more than a thousand years. While it was calling me too, I wasn't entirely clear on why. I simply knew that the pilgrimage was giving me a way to move into my next chapter and a chance to be with Juliet. Good enough reasons, no? Only later, with a bit of distance and discernment would I grow to understand the deeper reasons. Only over time would my relationship with my spiritual self begin to unfold. I began walking Camino thinking that this was a mother-daughter journey. But somewhere along The Way, I ended up as a faithful pilgrim.

Camino—and that's my shorthand throughout the book—is also called The Way of St. James because the faithful believe that relics of St. James himself are encased in a silver reliquary located in the crypt of Santiago's cathedral. I didn't realize before I left home that Santiago literally means Saint James, *Iago* being the Spanish name for James. Today, Saint James is still the patron saint of Spain. Paintings of Santiago Peregrino—St. James the *Pilgrim*—with his long brown robe, floppy hat, staff, and scallop shell are found in Spanish churches and convenience stores alike.

In modern-day Spanish vernacular, the common name for the Milky Way is El Camino de Santiago, inspired by the dust kicked up from pilgrims' feet. It gives you an idea of how the deep mysticism around Camino has transcended our vocabulary beyond religion and faith.

Over the centuries, the pilgrimage to Santiago fell in and out of popularity. Remarkably, though, it has endured over time. Camino was celebrated during medieval times and blessed by Popes who used the promise of a spiritual reward to feed souls and church coffers at the same time.

As with other Catholic pilgrimages, peregrinos would earn an "indulgence" when they received their Compostela or diploma at the end of the pilgrimage. As a lapsed Catholic and no expert on Catholic doctrine, I knew that if I received my Compostela in Santiago, it would not serve as a get-into-heaven-free pass, but I did hope that it would count for something. Perhaps an asterisk next to my name when St. Peter performed his background check.

When I started reading about Camino, I found its connection to the Knights Templar to be quite mysterious, like living in a Dan Brown novel. During the Middle Ages, at their height of power, the Knights Templar protected pilgrims along The Way. During this time, grand cathedrals were erected, "hospitals" to care for pilgrims were built, and services for pilgrims were sanctioned along the route.

Recently Camino has again enjoyed a surge in popularity, perhaps due to our yearning to tap into an ideal bigger than ourselves or thanks to Hollywood movies like *The Way* starring Martin Sheen.

While El Camino de Santiago is an ancient Catholic pilgrimage, you don't have to be Catholic nor deeply religious to walk it. We met peregrinos who walked for many reasons. Some of our fellow pilgrims were looking for a spiritual journey while others were on a more secular adventure. I met pilgrims who were walking and grieving. Some people walked to remember; others walked to forget.

Each year, approximately 200,000 walkers, cyclists, and a few pilgrims with donkeys set out with their own reasons to walk Camino. I wonder if, like me, their reasons looked different when they reached Santiago than when they began.

One thing that was certain was that we were all searching for inspiration along the same path and propelled toward the same single-minded destination—Santiago de Compostela, approximately 800 kilometers or 500 miles away.

In the mountain village of O Cebreiro, I picked up a prayer card in the ninth-century church that anchored the village, reportedly one of the oldest churches on Camino. A man by the name of Fraydino wrote the Pilgrim's Prayer that so eloquently sums up the power of Camino.

"Although I may have traveled all the roads,
Crossed mountains and valleys from east to west
If I have not discovered the freedom to be myself,
I have arrived nowhere.

"Although I may have shared all of my possessions
With people of other languages and cultures;
Made friends with pilgrims of a thousand paths,
Or shared albergue with saints and princes,
If I am not capable of forgiving my neighbor tomorrow,
I have arrived nowhere.

"Although I may have carried my pack from beginning to end
And waited for every pilgrim in need of encouragement,
Or given my bed to one who arrived later than I,
Given my bottle of water in exchange for nothing;
If upon returning to my home and work,
I am not able to create brotherhood
Or make happiness, peace and unity,
I have arrived nowhere.

"Though I may have had food and water each day
And enjoyed a roof and shower every night;

Or may have had my injuries well-attended,
If I have not discovered in all that the love of God,
I have arrived nowhere.

"Although I may have seen all of the monuments
And contemplated the best sunsets;
Although I may have learned a greeting in every language
Or tasted the clean water from every fountain;
If I have not discovered who is the author
Of so much free beauty and so much peace,
I have arrived nowhere.

"If from today I do not continue walking your path,
Searching and living according to what I have learned;
If from today I do not see in every person, friend or foe
A companion on the Camino;
If from today I cannot recognize God,
The God of Jesus of Nazareth
As the one God in my life,
I have arrived nowhere."

Before I left for Spain, I spent weeks reading, provisioning, and praying. I wasn't very good at praying, so I downloaded a book on how to pray to get better connected to my faith. I thought, how lame not to know how to pray. I even took notes on how to talk to God and *be specific* in my conversations. Hard as I tried, I was ashamed about the fact that I was on a spiritual pilgrimage and that my faith would be deemed lacking.

Over time, I began to understand that what I needed was just a little faith. How encouraging to know that I wasn't being judged on having enough faith, but on whether I had any faith at all.

My faith began to wash over me like a big wave. It took me by surprise and overwhelmed me, even if it was just a proverbial mustard seed. It was a healthy and reassuring reminder that small steps, small intentions, and a small amount of faith was all that was needed.

STATUE OF THE VIRGIN MARY

---------- Chapter 4 ----------

RESILIENCE

If you're going through hell, keep going.
~ Winston Churchill

Juliet and I flew to Barcelona in early June, where we spent a few days in one of Europe's signature cities. From the balcony of our apartment on Sicilia Street, we peered into the neighboring gardens below us. We watched as kids passed a soccer ball in the local schoolyard during recess, and our front door led straight into the still-unfinished Sagrada Familia, just one block away. Designed by Catalon architect Antoni Gaudi, the basilica looked more like a tourist attraction than a house of worship. It anchored the neighborhood with its sheer enormity, its expressive spires, and three facades filled with religious carvings. It was like a Where's Waldo search for Roman Catholic iconography.

As Juliet and I explored Barcelona, we lost count of the Catalon independence flags hanging from hundreds of wrought-iron city balconies. An anti-establishment sentiment was on the lips of every Catalonian. Juliet struck up conversations with the locals, including a taxi driver who complained in rapid-fire Spanish that the government in Madrid took all the revenue from prosperous Barcelona. Few of the funds were returned, fueling local defiance in favor of Catalonian independence.

Sitting high on a hill overlooking Barcelona, Juliet and I smiled for selfies in front of whimsical buildings, sculptures, and mosaics in Gaudi's Parc Guell. We lunched at café counters and ogled the wares of the fishmongers, butchers, fruit vendors, and spice peddlers at La Boqueria, one of Europe's most famous food markets. We ambled down Las Ramblas, the tree-lined artery through the Old Gothic Quarter of Barcelona to the Mediterranean Sea where Juliet took a late-afternoon dip while I people-watched.

As good as all this sounds, I was wracked with worry. All I wanted to do was begin walking. I was fighting to endure what felt like an endless period of waiting. Waiting to walk. I was not good at this in-between time, too ripe for second-guessing and worry. As I got older, I wasn't rolling with the punches nor dealing with disappointment as well as I had in the past. I needed to do a better job at adapting to whatever was tossed my way. I was working hard to adopt a more positive, resilient mindset.

But I wasn't there yet. In fact, I was sleeping only every other night despite the Tylenol PM in my med kit. I laid awake and grilled myself. Had I made the right decision to leave my job? Would I be able to walk 500 miles, especially with so little sleep? Even if I could handle the physical challenge, would I hate the journey—for whatever reason? Would my relationship with Juliet deteriorate instead of deepen?

Women are champions at worrying. It colors our worlds and our lives. We carry fear and worry around on our sagging shoulders; we sleep with it or don't sleep because of it. We worry about our children, our parents, our weight, our jobs, our friendships and marriages. We scrutinize, internalize, and in some cases, become paralyzed with worry, unable to see, let alone take, the next step. When we explore why women may not be natural risk-takers, I suspect that part of it is the bad habit of letting fear and worry travel with us in the many decisions that we make or don't make.

I had perfected the skill of worrying when Juliet was diagnosed with anorexia at 16. What had started as an effort to slim down and get in shape turned into an obsession and an increasingly rigid set of rules around food. Juliet lost weight and developed habits that worried Rick and me. We visited the pediatrician to make sure that Juliet's weight loss wasn't too much, too fast. Next, we saw a nutritionist to be sure that she was making healthy food choices. As she continued to restrict her diet and lose too much weight, we consulted with a national eating disorder clinic. They diagnosed Juliet with anorexia.

Our family spent the next several months—the summer before Juliet was scheduled to leave for her year in Spain—working with a team of medical practitioners and nutritionists trying to get Juliet's attitude toward food back into balance. There were painful and tearful stages of denial and belligerence. Juliet was so angry. She was angry at us, but mostly she was angry at herself and afraid that she may have hijacked her dreams to study in Spain.

Rick and I weren't ready to close the door on Spain, but we needed to be sure that Juliet would be healthy and safe 3,500 miles away. Juliet spent the whole summer doing what she was told—not easy for our strong-willed girl—and, as a result of her hard work, we decided she was healthy enough to spend her senior year with a Rotary family in Spain. While Juliet would still be dealing with eating issues in Spain, we didn't have to pick up a million pieces of our daughter, shattered like a mirror on the floor, by saying no.

Five years later, Juliet was in Spain again, this time with me as a companion. After a few days in Barcelona, we took a train to Pamplona, the city famous for the running of the bulls. In Pamplona, we hopped on a bus to St. Jean Pied-de-Port. Finally, we arrived at the gateway of the Camino Frances, our starting point for walking Camino.

There are many Camino routes: The Chemin de Puy in France. The coastal and rugged Camino del Norte. The Camino Primativo and Camino Portugues beginning in Lisbon and traveling through Porto on the way to Santiago.

For many, Camino begins as soon as you step out your front door. Before I left my company, a Dutch colleague shared that his mother had walked Camino, beginning at her home near Amsterdam. Every year for a week at a time, she invited a friend or a relative to walk with her, picking up each time where she left off. My colleague's mother died several years ago and his greatest regret, he told me softly, was that he was always too busy to take a week to walk Camino with her.

When Juliet and I arrived in the picturesque St. Jean Pied-de-Port, the cobblestone streets were filled with pilgrims. We needed only to see the hiking boots and hear the tap of the walking sticks to know that we were in the right place to begin. We pilgrims were all easy to spot with our backpacks and our scallop shells, the symbol of Camino. The symbolism of the scallop shell served as a fitting metaphor for the many roads that lead to Santiago de Compostela, just as the many grooves of the scallop shell converge at the tip.

Juliet and I picked up our Pilgrim's Credential on the rue de Citadelle. In a nondescript room, three volunteers stood behind folding tables where they welcomed peregrinos from all over the world. Our credential became our passport to inexpensive lodging and pilgrims' meals along the way. The credential's blank pages were both daunting and promising. When we arrived in Santiago, the pages would be filled with so many colorful stamps of our stops at albergues that they would hang off the end of the page.

Maps of routes and Camino-related posters covered the walls in the Pilgrims' Office. I paid special attention to the weather monitors that warned of coming rain and wind in the Pyrenees. In fact, it was hard to tear my thoughts away from the weather forecast.

A basket of scallop shells sat below a sign that requested donations in French, German, Spanish, and English. Some of the shells were painted with the Cross of St. James; all came with a piece of twine strung through a hole in the tip for tying to your pack. Juliet and I had brought our own scallop shells to Spain, so we left the box for other pilgrims. We had picked up our grey scallop shells on the sands of Assateague Island where we spent many happy family times.

On our first day of walking, we set out early in the morning from St. Jean. I had scouted the path out of town the night before and said a little prayer that our first day of walking would be a good day. Our destination was the Refuge Orisson, a welcome resting place on the French side of the Pyrenees' crossing. Just beyond Orisson—on the Spanish side of the mountains—was the village of Roncesvalles, my personal "proving point."

I figured that if we could make the crossing and get to the Augustinian monastery in Roncesvalles, I would be good from there on out. But the fact that the forecast was calling for bad weather in the mountains became one more reason not to sleep. I had been warned about pilgrims getting lost in whiteout conditions, taking a fall into a ravine, or making a fateful misstep at 4,300 feet.

Stepping away from my constant companion—worry—was a big assignment for me. I kept repeating to myself that worrying was praying for what you don't want. Intellectually I understood that worrying was not helping, but it felt impossible to shake. This step of the journey was incredibly hard for me.

As it turned out, Juliet and I walked out of St. Jean under a light fog on a paved road that led up into the Pyrenees. We eventually turned off the road and onto rutted, stone-filled pathways that cut across rocky fields and small farms. Griffin vultures caught updrafts high above these lush green valleys, and after three hours of climbing, we reached the Refuge Orisson.

We were met by a lively mix of languages on the deck. Peregrinos from around the world chattered excitedly, introducing themselves and enjoying the stunning views that overlooked a green patchwork of farm fields. The tiny smidge of buildings in the distance was the village of St. Jean where our day had begun.

After what would become a daily routine of showering and washing our sweaty clothes by hand, we could look forward to a communal dinner served early by Spanish standards but at a good time for tired peregrinos who would be shooed out bright and early the next morning.

We enjoyed a delicious meal of stewed chicken and rice, followed by several rounds of post-prandial songs. The long wooden tables were filled with French, Swedes, Koreans, a Japanese couple celebrating their second wedding anniversary, an enthusiastic Belgian, and a smattering of English speakers. The meal was a lovely introduction to a community of people with whom we would walk some or all of the way. Finally I slept.

COMMUNAL TABLE AT THE REFUGE ORISSON

Chapter 5

COMMUNITY

Friendship is born at that moment when one person says to another, "What! You too? I thought I was the only one."

~ C.S. Lewis

We woke up above the clouds. After a breakfast of coffee and toast, we began walking early and were joined by Marvin, a teenaged Swede walking the Camino with his 80-year-old grandmother, Anna. Anna had walked Camino at least twice before. Today she was skipping the rigorous climb across the Pyrenees, so Marvin had asked to walk with us. It turned out that Anna didn't make it all the way to Santiago on this trip, but Juliet and I saw Marvin many times again along The Way.

Finally, I was getting a handle on what to expect. The days crossing the Pyrenees, which I had anticipated with worry and sleepless nights, turned out to be two of my favorites. Mist clung to the valleys as we climbed through high-mountain pastures. The bleating of sheep and the bells around their necks filled each day with both sight and sound. I was delighted, no matter how many cow patties and horse droppings I stepped around. Basque shepherds with black berets watched over their flocks from lookout points on the bluffs. At one point, a herd of sheep raced hurriedly down the hillside toward what we assumed was their lunch.

Quite unexpectedly, we crested a hill and came across a young man selling juices, local cheese, and hard-boiled eggs, good fuel for pilgrims. He manned the first of many homemade concession stands we would encounter along The Way, often coming upon them at a moment when we needed them most.

The border from France into Spain is marked only by an ancient stone marker with the word Navarra carved onto it. This is the gateway not only into Spain but into Basque County. There was no immigration control and no request for papers.

Five and a half hours after leaving the Refuge Orisson, we walked into Roncesvalles. I was now enchanted by the rhythm of each day, and my confidence that I could handle the physical challenge of Camino was growing. Familiar faces from the Refuge Orisson joined new pilgrims who made the crossing from St. Jean in one day instead of two. It was close quarters among the 180 beds in the 13th-century Augustinian monastery in Roncesvalles. I would learn that night and many nights thereafter to tolerate, even appreciate, everything from snoring and farting to the many, many hairy backs bunking nearby.

Juliet wasn't interested in the church services, but attending mass became a welcome, even necessary, part of my Camino routine. Old Spanish women, their heads covered in black lace veils, sat in pews next to pilgrims wearing hiking boots and fast-wicking shirts. It occurred to me only weeks later that all of the masses I attended but one were spoken in Spanish. Even in another language, the message was clear: you are not alone on your journey back to your faith. After this mass, the priest called all of the pilgrims to the front of the church and personally blessed our Caminos. This would happen many times and, each time, I was grateful, and sometimes even greedy, for the blessing.

People were friendly and interested in getting to know one another. Wandering around during our free time, I came across Anthony perched on a wall and sketching the monastery. An architectural conservationist and English lord, Anthony was walking a stretch of Camino with his adult daughter, Rachel. With her shock of lavender hair, Rachel was easy to spot on the trail. I remembered our introduction around the dinner tables at Orisson the night before. When I told Rachel I wasn't sleeping, she gave me a homemade mixture of orange and lavender oils that offered some peace of mind. I appreciated the gesture, an early example of the giving culture of Camino.

The heavy weather that had kept me awake with worry finally arrived on our way out of Roncesvalles. Only later did we learn that two pilgrims crossing the Pyrenees during that time lost their way in the fog and died. A German couple related a harrowing story of a storm that hit the mountains and how they were stranded in a small hut used for emergency shelter at the top of the pass. I was reminded that no journey is without risk, and the risk accompanying this journey was not completely benign.

Just beyond the village of Roncesvalles, buckets of rain were falling. We dodged puddles on a muddy path alongside the Arga River, which had jumped her banks and was raging only a few steps away. I had debated about whether to bring both hiking boots and trail runners, finally deciding that anything that would protect my feet deserved a place in the pack. Carrying the extra weight was worth it if it saved my feet from blisters or sloppy conditions. Now I was happy to have my hiking boots which, while not completely waterproof, offered protection from the wet and slippery scree on the path.

Juliet and I walked in the pouring rain and talked with many people, most of whom were a mix of European nationalities. More Spanish walk Camino than any other nationality, but the Irish are regulars on the trail as well. Considering the proximity of Camino to Ireland, their national penchant for hill walking, and the fact that Camino is a Catholic pilgrimage, it isn't hard to understand.

I was continually surprised and delighted by the convivial Irish walkers I met. They would greet each other warmly and, in their fast-paced brogue, try to determine how they might be related to one another. Since I have Irish roots, I wondered if I were related too. The good nature of the Irish had a long-lasting influence on me.

During these early Camino days, Juliet and I found ourselves forming what would become long-lasting friendships. Juliet introduced me to Chuck, a retiree from Belfast who led leadership programs for Irish youth. Chuck talked about growing up in the 1970s in Belfast, a city torn apart by the civil war in Northern Ireland. He had dedicated his career to teaching Irish youth how to solve problems not by throwing fists and bombs, but through coalition building and civil discourse. I was fascinated by his colorful stories and his animated way of sharing a personal history very different than my own.

Like the Irish, the Dutch have a tradition of adventure and intellectual curiosity. Juliet and I found ourselves walking with Caroline, on sabbatical from her job as a city planner in Amsterdam. She and I are the same age, walked at the same pace, and were remarkably compatible. The fact that I had been to Amsterdam many times for work and knew the city well gave us a starting point for building an enduring friendship. Caroline walked in tights and a dress, and

had a down jacket that disappeared into her ul-
tralight pack. She and I spent many hours sorting
through our lives and enjoying an easy kinship. A
rain-soaked walk into Pamplona cemented my
friendship with both Chuck and Caroline, two
friends who deeply touched my Camino journey.

Camino friendships are forged by the intensity of
the journey and the communal experience of sharing
food, lodging, and conversation. No matter what
your nationality, your background, or political dispo-
sition, Camino has a way of reminding you that we
are all members of the same community.

Kumbaya aside, we were only a few days into our
pilgrimage and Juliet and I had been arguing on and
off as we slogged our packs through the rain. We
had exchanged angry words one evening as we tried
to find common ground. We both had a tendency
toward bossiness, so finding equal footing was difficult. We barked at each other, and I hoped that our
relationship would survive the walk.

At the time, we still had more than 30 days of
walking ahead of us, perhaps even 40 days of walking five to seven hours a day to reach Santiago. This
trip was meant to bring us together, not drive a
wedge between us.

When we finally dragged our sore feet and soaked
packs into Pamplona, we were happy to pay the high
price of 18 euros for pods at a newer albergue. The
proprietor boasted of a machine washer and dryer as

well as the best showers in Pamplona. For this night, at least, we wouldn't have to wash our clothes by hand and hope they would dry by morning. This was the first and only time I slept in a pod with a curtain I could close for privacy. Included was a small lock-box for personal belongings and sockets by the pillow for charging phones and iPods. I fancied myself sleeping in an oval-shaped dresser drawer that could be opened and closed just like my bedroom dresser at home.

Pamplona is an old walled city with great charm and Spanish lore, but my immediate destination after securing lodging was the 15th-century Catholic church, where I needed to say a prayer to the Virgin Mary for patience and strength. The church, the Catedral de Santa Maria, was fittingly named in honor of Mary, who was quickly becoming my confessor.

I had a little cry about how lost I felt on my birthday. Yes, it was my birthday.

After a few tears of self-indulgence and my prayers to Mary, I found my way to a Camino shop where I bought a pair of zip-off pants to replace ones I had left behind in the women's shower in Roncesvalles. After only a few days, I had already lost several items I had painstakingly selected for my journey. Losing one out of only three pairs of pants you packed sharpens your daily routine.

As a birthday gift to myself, I purchased a small yellow and blue Camino pin, which I attached to my white hat. This pin continues to be a modest but colorful reminder of my days as a pilgrim.

Birthdays are moments in time that beg reflection, and I was struggling. I wondered, am I happy with who I am at age 52? Where am I at in this point of my life? I didn't know if I was experiencing a midlife crisis, but I did know that I was missing Rick and not happy to be spending my birthday without him. Juliet and I were not having an easy time of it, and I worried about how things might worsen over the next days and weeks.

When I returned to the albergue from my shopping, Juliet, Caroline, and Chuck were waiting in the common room with a birthday cake and candles. They sang happy birthday, and we headed down the cobblestone streets in search of pinchos, a Basque form of tapas. We found a small restaurant open to the street where we could purchase a plate of pinchos and glass of wine for two euros or $2.50. An inviting and elaborate selection of pinchos were displayed behind the glass counter, making it easy to select everything from anchovies and baccalau to serrano ham with roasted red peppers. Skewered with a toothpick and served on a slice of bread, we placed order after order, sampling whatever looked appealing and washing it down with a glass of the local vino tinto.

Juliet, wanting as much as I did to set straight the argument from the night before, wrote me a lovely birthday note:

To Mom on her 52nd birthday:

I didn't want to write you a card on one of the tattered pages I'd ripped out of my journal, so here is the title page from my favorite book, Breath, the title itself a convenient reminder of the most vital of ingredients for our lives.

We've just finished our fourth day on the Camino and I spent a lot of time today thinking about the promise we made last night: to leave all the shit we've worried about behind and just focus on the walk. It's a very good goal I think, and we can work to help each other as our journey continues.

Like you said last night, I only get one mom. The mom I got is charismatic, strong-willed, warm-hearted, intelligent, and loving. I'm so glad I have the mom that I do.

Happy birthday, may your next year be less rainy than these last few days and more enlightening than you could wish for.

My pen is running out of ink and I owe you one drawing.

Love you,

J

More and more of our Camino companions stopped by to wish me a happy birthday, including Marvin and Anna, who serenaded me in Swedish. We were only four days into our walk and already we were becoming a community of friends and, in some cases, a Camino family.

LADIES NIGHT AT THE
CASA BANDERAS, VILACHÁ

———— Chapter 6 ————

TRUST

Trust yourself. You know more than you think you do.

~ Benjamin Spock

On Camino, we followed a collection of yellow arrows and scallop shells to find our way. We had rudimentary maps, but they fell plenty short of a GPS to tell us when to turn. As many pilgrims do, we relied on John Brierley's book, *A Pilgrim's Guide to the Camino de Santiago*. Brierley's indispensable guide provides recommended daily routes, distances between villages, topographical maps, and the locations of albergues and cafés. But mainly we looked for the yellow arrows that marked the way and had to trust that those arrows would be there when we needed them. Sometimes we had to look up to find our arrows on the side of buildings; sometimes they were at our feet. Some of the signs were formal and official looking while others were spray painted on a rock or the side of a tree. I found following these arrows to be part of the magic of Camino.

First, the yellow arrows served as a reassurance that we were on the right path. If I didn't see a yellow arrow for a kilometer or so, one would appear right when that kernel of uncertainty was settling in. I was grateful that getting lost on Camino was difficult—not impossible but also not common. Juliet and I did get lost once after we missed an arrow in the predawn darkness. We soon backtracked and found our way to the first coffee of the day after a short detour.

I hate getting lost. For me, it's an incredible waste of time. But you learn on Camino to let certain stuff go. Namely control. Even I was learning to trust that everything would work out in the end, that I would find a yellow arrow to point the way when I needed it. I had to trust that a warm welcome would be waiting no matter what time I arrived at our destination. One late afternoon we came across a beautiful young Belgian woman offering free hugs as the antidote to a long day of walking. Talk about a warm welcome.

I also had to trust that there would be a shower and an available bed at a local albergue to rest our weary bodies. Albergues, ranging from a few beds to hundreds, were lodgings available only to pilgrims.

We regularly exchanged information with other pilgrims about albergues on Camino. In fact, the condition of albergues ran second only to the constant conversation about sore feet.

"Don't stop at the first albergue in the next village. Even if you are tired, keep pressing on," came a message passed back along the chain of walkers. "We heard that several pilgrims were bitten by bed bugs and had to be fumigated when they reached their next destination."

Further into the journey, Juliet experienced the humiliation of bed bugs when she and her pack were quarantined at an albergue near Astorga. She was given a spare pair of shorts and an oversized shirt and made to wait like a naughty child sent to the time-out corner until the hospitaleros were satisfied with her pack and penance. Thankfully, I never had an up-close-and-personal run-in with these critters.

Another important piece of information that we discussed among our small group was the strength of the Wi-Fi signal at any given stopping point. While traditionalists discourage modern devices, we were insistent about seeking out good Wi-Fi. We used Wi-Fi apps to communicate with our families back home and with each other on the trail. Most of us relied on *What's App* to send messages, make occasional phone calls, and post blogs, which I did with great delight each day. Friends from back home followed my journey and cheered me on. We maintained a careful balance between staying loosely tethered to loved ones back in the States and immersing ourselves in the experience of the moment.

Many albergues were run by religious orders, parishes, and confraternities. Confraternities are organizations of Christian volunteers dedicated to charitable work. It wasn't uncommon for us to bunk in a monastery or convent. The albergues, both the religious and secular ones, shared a standard set of rules. Typically, we could stay for one night only and had to be on our way in the morning by 8 a.m. Some accommodations included a communal meal and some, like the monastery in Roncesvalles, had a curfew and locked the doors at 10 p.m. The curfew usually wasn't a problem for weary pilgrims.

As we checked into each night's albergue, Juliet and I got our passports stamped with their unique and colorful insignia. Under the stamp, the hospitalero wrote the date to verify our passage. These stamps became especially important to have on the final 100 kilometers from Sarria into Santiago, the minimum needed to earn a Compostela. Traffic on the path picked up on this final stretch. During the summer months, groups of Spanish students walk in order to list a Compostela on their resumes right next to an internship or computer course.

During ancient times, pilgrims were expected to rely only on donations for their lodging and food. They had to trust that they would find goodwill and hospitality along The Way.

As modern-day pilgrims, we paid 10 euros, on average, for a bed. Beds came with a pillow and sometimes a blanket, but we were expected to have our own sheet or sleeping bag. Dating back to the early history of Camino, some of the religious albergues were donativo, which meant that you paid only what you could afford.

Everywhere I turned, I was reminded that Camino was not just a walk but a pilgrimage. My pilgrimage. But what does it mean to be a pilgrim? I didn't know. I understood that I was walking an ancient path to a holy place, but it would take time to understand that I was traveling through an inner landscape to somewhere new as well.

Practically speaking, Juliet and I were getting the rhythm of the journey by the fourth and fifth day. Since Juliet walked faster than I did, we would often have to make plans about meeting up at the end of the day, selecting a destination we hoped would be impossible to miss. As women, we were vigilant about personal safety and careful to not walk alone for long stretches.

While I never felt unsafe on Camino, we heard a tragic story of an American woman from Phoenix, Denise Thiem, who disappeared that same year near the city of Astorga. Sadly, her body was found after a five-month search. She died at the hands of a local man who had been known to harass pilgrims on a section of Camino near his home. Despite this isolated incident, Camino is relatively crime free. Other pilgrims are usually in sight, and our Camino community looked out for one another.

Everything along the route is set up to service pilgrims. In turn, pilgrims keep many of the small Spanish towns in business. They cater to the need for restaurants, lodging, and supplies.

But during the day, the small villages along the route feel nearly deserted. These are ancient and sometimes forgotten towns, removed from the modern-day world. I thought, how many places can you still visit that feel like a step back in time? My mind wandered through the ruins of crumbling stone buildings and narrow medieval streets that opened onto quiet village plazas. A few older folks watched the world go by from benches that sat shaded from the brutal Spanish sun. I wondered how many pilgrims they had watched walk through their town. Had they ever walked Camino themselves?

On Camino, as in life, I couldn't see around every corner and didn't know what waited for me in the next town. Many days, I didn't know where I would sleep for the night or whether I would find a small store that was open so that I could provision an empty pack. I was beginning to practice my faith, both spiritually and pragmatically, learning to trust that everything would work out, that I would find a yellow arrow to point the way when I needed it the most.

COLLECTION OF ARROWS AND SCALLOP
SHELLS THAT MARKED THE WAY

—————— Chapter 7 ——————

SIMPLICITY

Carry only what you need.

I love the concept of simplicity and carrying only what you need. For decades, I have traveled around the world with only one carry-on bag. It doesn't matter if I am traveling for three days or three weeks, I carry what I need in one bag. Traveling light forces me to make strategic packing choices, balancing the freedom of minimalism with the need to be ready for every occasion. Traveling light is liberating, but it requires a certain amount of "letting go." Given that I would have to shoulder the weight of everything I packed, provisioning and packing for Camino took me several weeks.

At the beginning of my journey, my Cabela's backpack weighed 18 pounds. Two friends who had walked Camino rummaged through my pack at the local Panera Bread, ditching "extras" they assured me I would not need. My pile of obsolescence included a few tops and all makeup. Despite their experienced recommendations, the lipstick and blush made the final cut and found a place in the pack.

I did learn, over time, what bits and pieces were left unused. I pared my pack down to 15 pounds by donating a few items to communal "take me" tables for other travelers. I left the never-opened blush behind in one albergue, hoping that a young peregrina would appreciate it for an unexpected date night.

Juliet's pack, on the other hand, weighed 30 pounds. She and I laughed about her being young, strong, and stupid. In addition to I-don't-know-what, she started out with her favorite book, *Breath*, and picked up *A Short History of Nearly Everything* by Bill Bryson in Hornillos del Camino. Think about it: *A Short History of Nearly Everything*. This book could moonlight as a door jam, thanks to its sheer heft. Let's just say that, while I was slower on the downhill, I could smoke Juliet on the ascents.

The most important belongings in my pack were all about my feet. What do you need the most to walk 500 miles? Strong, healthy feet. I agonized over the decision between hiking boots and trail runners. I brought both and was happy I did.

Sticks or no sticks? I practiced first with one and then with two after a friend suggested that walking with only one leaves you lopsided. In addition to Caroline, my red walking sticks, one purchased at REI, the other at Walmart, turned out to be my best friends on Camino. Leaving them behind was never an option.

Rain gear, earplugs, clothespins, sink stopper, laundry detergent, headlamp, fanny pack, first aid supplies, knee support, whistle, synthetic and merino wool socks, and a hat.

A word about me and hats. I love hats and wear them all the time. My hats range from summer straw hats to fashionable hats worthy of Derby Day picnics. My collection of winter hats makes me easy to spot on the ski slopes. I share a penchant for wearing exceptional hats with the African American ladies at Sunday services and the late fiercely feminist New York Congresswoman, Bella Abzug. Getting the right hat for my 500-mile trek was a chore. I tested hats with brims too big and others too shallow. Finally, I found a simple white cloth hat at a local Target. It was packable and had the right-sized brim. As I packed, I hoped the hat would hold its shape and wondered what color it would be at the end of Camino. I suspected that it wouldn't be white.

Clearly, what went into the pack was hugely important. The process of stripping life down to the bare necessities forces a conversation about what you can't live without. And what was central to me was different than what was crucial to Juliet. For me, everything had to serve multiple purposes. I was willing to leave questionable items behind. But the lipstick went along.

You pay a price for what you carry, on Camino as in life. Five days into our journey, it was not surprising to see knee supports on the young and old alike. Pilgrims could be found sitting along the path, on rocks and in café chairs administering to aching bodies and sore feet. There was a certain etiquette about how much foot first aid was acceptable at a café table. I had no blisters but was happy for a tennis ball to roll underneath my sore arches as homespun physical therapy. Everyone was finding his or her own best pace; some people charged ahead and others moved more slowly, but we were all feeling the rigors of walking for up to seven hours each day.

On our way out of Pamplona, we decided to take a taxi part of the way. The weather was still miserable so we gave ourselves permission to walk for only a half day. We found a taxi driver willing to take us to the Church of Saint Mary of Eunate by way of the Alto del Perdon, a scenic, high point in the hills outside of Pamplona.

Juliet and the taxi driver chatted in Spanish like old friends. It's no surprise that the Spanish love to talk. Big issues and little ones, weather and politics, gossip and family—anything is fair game for an opening conversation with a Spaniard. Juliet thrived on these animated chats with everyone from taxi drivers to shopkeepers. She loved the compliments about how well she spoke Spanish and her slightly Galician accent.

At the end of the ride, our driver gave Juliet the gift of a new walking stick. She had been walking with a large tree branch that she found along the path. As we gathered our packs from the back of the van, he removed Juliet's walking stick and broke it in half over his knee, replacing it with one left behind in his taxi by another peregrino. My jaw dropped as they parted with hugs and laughter.

The Alto del Perdon is famous for its enormous wind turbines and iron sculptures of Camino pilgrims. Pilgrims on foot and riding donkeys lean into the wind on their way to Santiago. Sitting high on a peak called the Mount of Forgiveness, the alto also offers sweeping views of the Basque Country. Local school children posed for photos with the wrought-iron pilgrims and, as we waited our turn, Juliet translated the Spanish inscription on one sculpture: "Where the way of the wind crosses the way of the stars."

While our views across the valley were socked in with fog, the wind was beginning to clear away the heavy weather as we drove down the mountain and headed into the valley for the Church of St. Mary of Eunate. Eunate was built in the 12th century in the shape of an octagon, part of the symbolism of the

Knights Templar. It's an ancient and moving place. The interior is stark and simple with a primitive statue of Mary and the baby Jesus serving as its focal point.

I didn't miss a chance to shoot Mary a prayer. I thought Mary would be inclined to hear a mother's plea for guidance. Mom to mom. She also embodied for me everything that is good and hopeful, giving me the confidence to continue when I was faced with my own limitations and fears.

At this point in our journey, Juliet moved in and out of our group, often preferring the company of new pilgrims she met each day. I mostly understood her interest in meeting new people, especially those with whom she could speak Spanish. After all, it was thanks to Juliet's outgoing personality that I had met Caroline and Chuck in the first place.

But I also had to recognize that Juliet's and my journeys were on two separate but parallel paths. Sometimes we would travel together and in lock step; at other times, we would only meet down the road at a preset time. We took the opportunity to be as close or as far away from each other as we needed to be, an interesting metaphor for what happens naturally between parents and their children as everyone grows up. I was not disappointed when we decided to part ways at various points, but I always wanted to know how and when we would meet up again.

The clearing clouds were promising to see as we walked the remaining kilometers to Puente La Reina, famous for its Romanesque Queen's Bridge. The albergue Jakue, with its sunlit terrace overlooking the banks of the River Arga, sat at the beginning of the town. We were now seeing many familiar faces, pilgrims young and old, who were on our same schedule—and conversations picked up where they left off. At dinner, with the Irish contingent around the table, I could understand only every third word of the good-natured banter. In a culture of talkers, conversations ranged from world politics to Spanish food and local wine to our feelings about the Camino journey itself. The conversation usually began and ended with the weather, but in between was a glorious romp about everything else.

Even this early on, the small towns that dotted our journey began to blur together. Each shared an elaborate stone church, most of which were built around 1500, that anchored the main plaza. You could not miss the Roman Catholic Church's message of wealth and power.

With thick walls, barrel naves, and stained-glass windows, these extraordinary churches, many of them built in the Romanesque style, towered over often unremarkable and modest rural villages. I often wondered what price the locals paid for such impressive gateways to heaven. At the same time, I loved the sense of history I found in these inspired masterworks.

After days of rain, we now enjoyed the simple pleasure of ideal walking weather—70 degrees and partly cloudy with a light breeze. While other pilgrims were usually in sight, the path was not too busy at this stage and, even when others were around, you could walk alone with your thoughts.

Typically, we began walking around 7:30 a.m., arriving at our destination tired but happy by 2 p.m. after walking an average of 15 miles a day. I loved this routine, as it left me with plenty of time in the afternoon for exploring, provisioning, and writing a blog so I could share the journey and remember its rich details. After we reached our day's destination and washed ourselves and our clothes, it was time to be social and lead the "café life" with lively conversations and vino tinto.

Since we were walking through Basque Country, Chuck and I discussed the separatist politics of the region. Coming of age in Belfast in the 1960s and 1970s, he had a very personal perspective on civil war. He had lost friends to the conflict and maintained a fiercely secular opinion on religion and politics. I was engrossed to hear this up-close-and-personal angle on conflict.

Our three-generation group now numbered eight. When the fastest walkers of the group arrived at our evening's weigh-station, we reserved a place for those walking at a slower pace. One day, our goal was to reach the Capuchin monastery in Estella where we would rest for the night.

The town of Estella is split by the river, so we ambled over to what appeared to be the livelier side of town for dinner. We wandered the warren of streets and finally found a restaurant on a plaza beginning to come to life with Spanish families. Spain's nocturnal culture often didn't jive with our early-to-bed, early-to-rise schedule. On many nights, we ate our dinner before the locals even ventured out for their evening of tapas, drinks, and socializing.

A sandwich board advertised a Menu de Peregrino, the simple staple meal of Camino, typically ten euros or a little more than $12 for a starter, main course, and dessert. And wine! In fact, the price didn't change no matter how much wine we drank. A bottle of the local vino tinto was left at the table with our meal and cheerfully refilled on many occasions. We had now passed from Pays Basque into Spain's predominant wine-making region and enjoyed the local Rioja.

One of the challenges of Camino is a diet heavy on carbohydrates. Finding fresh vegetables on local menus was hard, so we stopped each day at small tiendas to provision fruit, tomatoes, nuts, and dark chocolate. I grew to love my breakfast routine of a tomato that I ate like an apple, along with a café con leche or two.

Sometimes we ate lunch at cafés along the route. At other times we ate out of our packs, finding a shady spot to rest along a river or by the edge of a farmer's field. It was always a treat when we climbed a steep rock and grass track to be surprised by a makeshift café set up at the top of the hill. The Irish enjoyed the cold beer while everyone did a foot check.

On our way out of Estella, we came across the famous wine fountain, the Fuente del Vino, where the monks continue a tradition from the 10th century of fortifying pilgrims with free wine. A popular stopping point on Camino, the sign suggested that we should have a good luck drink for the long journey to Santiago. Since it was still before 9 a.m., Juliet and I had an obligatory sip and mugged for the camera.

A band of German brothers wearing "Five Brothers to Santiago" T-shirts were noisily cooking their dinner of omelets and potatoes when we arrived at the colorful Casa de Austria albergue in Los Arcos. After washing our clothes and wringing them out with an old-fashioned hand roller, we sorted out a bottle of red wine and sat on the second-story balcony watching a late afternoon storm roll in. Then, as soon as our Camino family had become comfortable with one another, the dynamic changed. In Logrono, we said a woeful good-bye to the Irish.

Tracy's Packing List: 18 pounds

Outerwear:
- ✓ Headlamp
- ✓ 2 walking sticks
- ✓ Sleeping bag liner and pillowcase
- ✓ Rain cover for pack
- ✓ Hiking boots (wear)
- ✓ Trail runners
- ✓ Keen sandals for after walking
- ✓ Two water bottles

Clothes:
- ✓ Rain jacket
- ✓ Fleece pullover
- ✓ 3 pair undies
- ✓ 2 long-sleeved walking shirts
- ✓ 1 tank top
- ✓ 1 T-shirt
- ✓ 2 light evening shirts
- ✓ 1 pair zip-off pants
- ✓ 1 pair walking capris
- ✓ Skort
- ✓ 2 bandanas
- ✓ 2 bras
- ✓ 3 pair socks
- ✓ Hat

Med Kit:
- ✓ Advil, Imodium, Tylenol PM
- ✓ Neosporin
- ✓ Compeed, Leukotape, Moleskin, Band-Aids

Sundries:
- ✓ Roll of TP
- ✓ Toothbrush/toothpaste
- ✓ Laundry liquid
- ✓ Deodorant
- ✓ 4 clothespins

- ✓ Small body wash
- ✓ Extra contacts, contact solution, and glasses
- ✓ Sunblock
- ✓ Lipstick and eyeliner
- ✓ Tweezers
- ✓ Nail clippers
- ✓ 3 emery boards
- ✓ Razor
- ✓ Comb
- ✓ Earplugs

Miscellaneous:
- ✓ Fast-drying towel
- ✓ Twist ties
- ✓ Safety pins
- ✓ 1 carabiner
- ✓ Whistle
- ✓ Adapter and plug
- ✓ Phone and charger
- ✓ Journal and 4 pens
- ✓ Brierley guidebook
- ✓ US passport and travel docs
- ✓ Camino passport
- ✓ Credit cards and money
- ✓ Rosary
- ✓ Sunglasses
- ✓ Extra plastic baggies
- ✓ My scallop shell

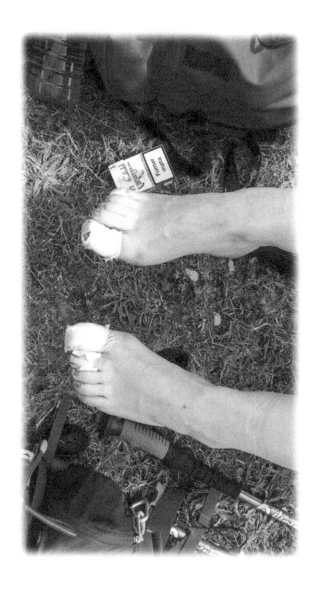

THANKFULLY NOT MY FEET!

---— Chapter 8 ——---

REFLECTION

Some people feel the rain. Others just get wet.

~ Roger Miller

One of the lessons that became abundantly clear on Camino was that the faster you go, the less time you have to think. It's so easy to get caught up in the to-do list of everyday life. In fact, I characterize my pre-Camino life as "all action, no reflection." If you're like me, you worry about whether you are making sound decisions as you race through life, decisions that are too often made without time for contemplation.

I love the fact that walking for long stretches demands that you slow down. Surviving 500 miles on foot compels you to set a measured pace. Interestingly, it must be your own pace and not one forced by someone else's stride. It doesn't take long to feel pretty uncomfortable by walking too fast or too slowly. Endurance walking is sustainable only when you settle into your own natural pace.

Once you let your body fall into its natural rhythm, it does its job automatically. You turn on the machine and it knows how to walk, thus freeing you up to think. Whether it boosts your mood, changes your scenery, or gets more blood pumping to your brain, long-distance walking also helps you to tap into thoughts that are buried so deeply that they are typically unavailable.

This methodical act of putting one foot in front of the other also seems to trigger creative thinking. A long list of distinguished writers, innovators, and composers used walking as a thinking tool. For example, Apple Inc. founder Steve Jobs was well known for his long walks around Silicon Valley. American poet Robert Frost wrote his finest poems after walks in the New England woods. Writer Charles Dickens, scientist Charles Darwin—the list of original thinkers who used walking to stoke their creative juices goes on and on.

Before I left the corporate world, I installed a standing desk in my office. I was tired of sitting for 10 hours a day and hoped I could burn a few more calories by standing instead of sitting. The man who next occupied my office removed it pretty quickly, but as I look back, the desk may have been a first small step out the door. Clearly, I didn't want to feel planted, and I wanted to keep moving. A long walk was just the ticket.

Almost to a person, the people I met on Camino were carving time out of their busy lives to sort out the answers to their innermost and private questions. To set out on Camino is to give yourself both permission and opportunity to have a conversation with yourself or with God about what is unresolved in your life.

All of us as pilgrims needed to set our own pace so we could find the answers we were seeking. In many cases, I suspect my fellow pilgrims already knew what they were looking for but needed affirmation, confidence, or perhaps a game plan in order to take their next step. In particular, I continued to come across many middle-aged women who were in search of an honest conversation with themselves. I'm not saying that the men walking Camino weren't also contemplative, but I particularly noticed women who, like me, had reached an intersection in their lives. They were using this journey to shine the spotlight on their own needs. Some were thinking about what to do now that their kids were grown. Others were reflecting on their marriages and asking themselves whether they were still in love.

I was thinking about many things. Where I wanted to find purpose in my work and what I wanted to do when I returned from Camino. During my early career, I had worked in Washington and thought I was destined to run for office. Did I still feel that passion? Was it still my dream to serve?

Sometimes in the morning, I would make a plan for my reflection for the day. I scheduled a long day across the hot Meseta to think about my childhood and try to conjure up long-buried memories. I liked to think I still had access to the rich memories that made up the fabric of my life but that I just needed a bit of time to unlock them.

Like so many others on Camino, I thought about my family and my marriage. I counted my lucky stars that I was happy in love. I believe that the most important decision you make in life is who you marry. I've been known to thank my husband Rick for choosing me as his companion in life. The fact that Rick was a full partner in my decision to trek Camino with Juliet is a good example of his support and deep understanding of me.

Several years ago, Rick and I began riding a tandem bicycle. Rick purchased it for my birthday, and it was my favorite birthday gift ever.

Many couples have a hard time keeping the peace on a tandem. It's true that it requires a lot of communication from the person pedaling in the front. Rick must tell me when to coast and when to pedal. I can't see the intersections and must be warned when we are banking a turn. On the other hand, I get great side views and can look up at the canopy for as long as I like. I occasionally pat Rick's sweaty back to thank him for being the big horse in the front.

Rick refers to our tandem bicycle as a marital aid. We have had some of our most touching and personal conversations on the tandem, biking past farm fields, talking about our aspirations and working out feelings that can be obscured by the busyness of day-to-day lives. When I told Rick that I would miss not having my best friend with me on Camino, he assured me that he would be there every step of the way. Just like always.

Being happy in love didn't mean that I didn't have a lot to sort through myself on Camino. For someone like me who likes to be in control, this trip was about learning to let go, to take each day as it comes. As a professional woman, I was also thinking about where to take my career next and where I might find inspiration when I plugged back into life after Camino. Walking at your own pace for five to seven hours a day puts you in touch with your body and mind, testing your stamina at the same time that it offers you the gift of time to think.

SUN-SOAKED STRETCH ACROSS THE MESETA

Chapter 9

BALANCE

Breathe. Let go. And remind yourself that this very moment is the only one you know you have for sure.

~ Oprah Winfrey

L ife is a constant struggle to stay in balance. We struggle with work-life balance, a balanced diet, and a careful balance between taking risks and pushing our boundaries versus the security of coloring within life's lines. They say that extremes are easy, and I think that's right. Striving for balance, that's the hard part, harder yet when you are living life large.

Moms in particular are constantly fighting a battle with balance, not only in managing the to-do list for ourselves and our families, making sure everyone gets what he or she needs, but also keeping our emotions in balance. We want our children to know our love balanced against our high expectations. We want them to benefit from our mistakes at the same time that we need them to experience independence and suffer failure. Personally, I was never afraid to fail, only afraid that I wouldn't try hard enough.

When I left my position after 10 years of 24/7, my tank was out of gas and I was feeling pretty out of balance. Camino was an opportunity for me to rebalance my priorities and, in this case, put my daughter and what this journey meant, both individually and to us as mother and daughter, in front of other needs.

But even on Camino, I struggled with balance. When did it make sense to walk together with Juliet and when apart? Would walking separately cause me to miss out on this opportunity to spend time with Juliet?

We all fall out of balance. The art of remaining upright and steady requires constant adjustment—sometimes big and sometimes subtle. I thought about how transitions and the in-between are especially unbalanced times in our lives. Juliet was in between childhood and adulthood, and I needed to let her find her own way. I was transitioning from being a mom to a fellow traveler and needed to lighten up.

Was everybody else on Camino struggling with balance, or was it only me?

One thing I did know was that my idea of balance was different than my daughter's. As a yoga enthusiast, Juliet understood that by pressing her big or little toe during tree pose, she could stay balanced. Wobbling is part of the process. In fact, balance can't happen by standing still. And it can't happen without full attention and focus. But balance in the bigger sense is not Juliet's long suit. Nor is taking anything but the hardest route. I asked Juliet to share thoughts on the topic:

By Juliet

I've never been a big fan of serenity. Outside the context of an occasional spa day, the idea of everything going according to plan and settling comfortably into contentment has never appealed to me.

My parents will be some of the first people to tell you that I have almost never done things the easy way. If there was a more complicated path, I was all over it before I even fully realized what that path would entail. I tend to throw myself into my decisions with characteristic abandon and little regard for long-term consequences. This doesn't mean I don't worry about things; in fact, I wrestle often with loud anxiety and even louder self-criticism. I just worry about everything while I'm already in the air instead of before jumping off the cliff.

Living my life by leaping feet-first into the next adventure has led to an extraordinary existence so far. I have lived on three continents, made countless friends across the globe, and gathered experiences that many people only dream of having.

I've certainly learned more about myself through struggle than I would have in a more serene environment. This is the reward I earn by gritting my teeth and shouldering through the rough times that are woven into all big adventures. Nothing great is easy. Nothing important is revealed from chasing the comfortable. By saying "what the hell, let's do it!" to the more unusual opportunities that come my way, I've sculpted my life into a series of steps that are far more interesting than any conventional path. In addition to having an excellent story to tell, I have a backlog of lessons that I carry with me into each new experience. A lesson most effectively learned is a lesson learned the hard way.

That being said, this chapter is about balance. I am not good at balance. I tend to swing wildly from one emotion to the next, and the balance of my lifestyle can be summed up by the phrase: "Sometimes I work out and eat salads. Other times I eat cupcakes and refuse to put on pants. It's called balance."

I've always been better at extremes, but that doesn't mean I'm not constantly striving to reach a better equilibrium between my unconventional lifestyle and my need for stability. I'm the first to jump into new and challenging situations, but I must consciously balance it out with the legwork that's involved. For example, I often procrastinate when I should be packing and preparing for a journey. I'm sure the only reason I packed early for the Camino trip was because of my mother's prodding. Nonetheless, I made some lists and gathered my gear, ensuring that I had everything I needed for the month-long trek.

I had to shoulder the extra weight of my pack that came in carrying all of the supplies I wanted to bring along. At one point during the hike, we all weighed our loaded packs on the albergue's scale; mine was twice the recommended weight of 15 pounds. Unlike my mother, who had down-sized as much as humanly possible in order to carry a lighter load, I refused to unload some of the items that added weight to my bag. Instead, I lugged that 30-pound backpack for 500 miles. The phrase Mom used was "young, strong, and stupid."

I definitely learned the hard way that I wouldn't need to carry items like my camp hammock or my three books during the entire Camino but, in my own way, I saw this as a vital lesson of my journey: Be careful what you carry because you're the one who shoulders it when all is said and done. This is the type of perspective on balance that I embrace: Challenge yourself and push through discomfort in order to grow but remember that all the hardship you invite will be left up to you to handle. It's no one's lesson but yours.

CLIMBING THE LONG STAIRCASE INTO
PORTOMARIN

— Chapter 10 —

GRATITUDE

Enough is as good as a feast.

~ Mary Poppins

For me, walking Camino was steeped in gratitude. I was so thankful for the opportunity to take this journey with Juliet. I was grateful that she said I could come along. I hoped that the shared experience would bring us closer through mutual respect, appreciation, and understanding. Our relationship had always been loving but not without hard edges. I hoped that, as two adults, we could buff those edges down.

In the meantime, I was on Camino learning how to appreciate the smallest gifts that each day offered. One gift was the quiet that gave me a chance to listen to my thoughts unfold. When I needed a break from the conversation in my head, I could listen to the birds waking up across the grasslands and, later, frogs peeping in a nearby canal.

The canal I have in mind eventually led to the home of Pepe in Espinosa del Camino, a village of 30 people and one lonely café. Pepe is a widower who ekes out a modest living by renting two rooms with bunk beds on the second floor of his home. He served us a lovely dinner of salad and paella, after which we took photos, sang songs, and learned about his collections of replica swords, crosses, and miniature soldiers. Since Pepe speaks only Spanish, Juliet translated as he led us around the house, telling stories and delighting in his audience.

We happened to be in Espinosa on the eve of the Summer Solstice, and I was grateful that I was spending it in the company of two Swedish women who sent us into the fields—and into a few private gardens—to pick seven kinds of flowers. We wove the flowers into wreaths and tied them into bundles with string. We placed the bundles under our pillows so that we would dream of love. That evening, Pepe enjoyed the company of eight women with flowers in their hair who sang and laughed over vino tinto.

Typically, our mornings began quietly as we organized our packs as noiselessly as possible and got on our way. Not this morning! Pepe had his own special way of waking his guests with bugles and military marches blaring through our quarters.

As an early riser and coffee-drinker, I was interested only in a caffeine fix for breakfast. I was grateful for the "Hobbit" tradition of second breakfast, which we would typically enjoy after several kilometers into the day's trek. By this time, we could always find a proper café with checked tablecloths and red chairs promising a café con leche and tortilla to fuel our bodies until lunch. Everyone seemed to love second breakfast, as the café chairs were filled with pilgrims now awake and ready for another day of walking.

We were on our way to Burgos, an historic Spanish city with an unforgettable Gothic cathedral that dominated the old quarter. After Pamplona, it was the next real city on our Camino, which meant that we would find better services here than what we had found in the smaller villages. The Museum of Human Evolution was high on Juliet's list, and seeing the grand Cathedral was high on mine. Burgos also was the home of El Cid and had been the seat of Franco's government until the end of the Spanish Civil War.

This larger city was a natural gathering place for peregrinos. We began seeing the familiar faces of pilgrims who had walked ahead or stayed in different towns along the way. Like a family reunion, pilgrims greeted each other as old friends, looking forward to a few days of rest and exploration.

That night, we paid five euros to stay in the municipal albergue with its 180 beds. That's right, five euros a night, the equivalent of $6.00. Munis are run by local governments and are often the most inexpensive lodging option. At 10:30 p.m., they lock the doors and don't reopen them until 6 a.m.

I can't say, however, I got much sleep at the muni. In the Burgos muni, I was unfortunately assigned a top bunk, which I tried to avoid at all of the albergues, largely due to middle-of-the-night visits to the loo. This muni had the highest bunk beds I had ever seen, and no one around me wanted to swap. So I spent a sleepless night glued in place, sure I was going to fall out of my bunk and break both my legs.

The room was big and the muni noisy. My fellow pilgrims created such an epic snoring racket that when I did sleep, I dreamed of dragons. I couldn't wrestle my way into my bag for my earplugs, mainly for fear of falling out of my high bunk. I vowed to think ahead about those earplugs the next time I slept in the same room as so many men.

As we set out for the village of Castrojeriz, our pre-dawn departure afforded a beautiful sunrise and the spectacular ruins of the 14th-century San Anton Monastery. As we rounded a bend in the road, I was gobsmacked by the appearance of the monastery, largely abandoned except for a small building on the property that housed a bare-bones albergue. A narrow road to Castrojeriz runs under a two-story portico of stone carvings connecting the ruin with the more modern world in its path.

Preparations were underway in Castrojeriz for the annual Garlic Festival that night. Juliet excitedly made plans to attend, buying a garlic bulb from the local tienda. At midnight, everyone would throw their garlic bulbs into an enormous bonfire and, with it, banish the demons from their lives. When Juliet learned that the doors of our albergue would be locked at 10 p.m. with no exceptions, she wore her disappointment for the rest of the day.

Her consolation prize was the sunrise over a new threshold. We were now crossing onto the Meseta, the arid high plains of northern Spain where we began walking at 6 a.m. each day and tried to arrive to our destination by noon. Even by the late morning hours, the treeless central plateau became unforgiving. I was grateful for a gentle breeze that kept us cool as the Spanish sun found her strength.

Because the landscape of the Meseta is flat and monotonous, it began the most emotional stretch of the journey. Many peregrinos believe that the Pyrenees test travelers physically, while the end of the journey through Galicia offers the most spiritual aspect of the walk. The middle of the journey is across the Meseta, which challenges pilgrims emotionally and reminds us all that we are there for a purpose and, whatever our purpose, we shouldn't waste the time we have given ourselves to think about it.

I was so thankful that my body was strong enough to walk 500 miles. And with no blisters. I watched fellow pilgrims become hobbled with injury and suffer blisters that took them out of the game. I took good care of my feet, but I suspect I was lucky, too. I bought my boots and trail runners a size larger than my normal size to account for the natural swelling that happens on a long-distance walk. My feet got tired and my sciatica would flare and hurt, but I stayed free of injury and grateful for it, too.

A short distance into the Meseta, our Camino family separated again. Our Swedish companions were looking for time alone to think about why they had come. One was trying to decide if she was still in love with her husband, and the other was trying to come to terms with a childhood filled with anguish and abuse.

At this point, Juliet, Caroline, and I also took the opportunity to see what it was like to walk alone. I was not happy about this, but I understood that getting the time and space we all needed to work on our own issues wasn't a bad idea. It was my turn to be alone with my own thoughts and see if I could come to conclusions about where I was at age 52 and where I wanted to go next. How lucky was I to have the opportunity to be unstuck from my job and look for a new way to use my professional gifts.

I appreciated this chance to practice my gratitude by thinking about my many blessings, both the blessings back home and the blessed beauty all around me. Spain is an exceptionally scenic country, and our ritual at the end of each day included curating photos of the lovely landscapes that etched our day. Remember the Pilgrim's Prayer? Fraydino talked about "so much free beauty," and I was truly grateful to be savoring each step as I walked through it.

Since we now had the lay of the land and were reassured about personal safety, I said to Juliet, "I will meet you in five days in Leon. Wait for me there." I knew she would move faster than I could walk and remain ahead of me. "App me every day to let me know that you are okay."

As I walked, I thought about all the things I loved about my daughter. Juliet is passionate and experiences life deeply. Her intellectual curiosity keeps her thinking, and her zest for adventure brought us to Camino. She got such joy out of speaking Spanish with the locals. In fact, the baker in Granon told me Juliet spoke better Spanish than most Spaniards.

Being a mom to both Juliet and Danny is a special gift.

We as mothers love many things about our children and have many wishes for them. I thought about what I wished for Juliet in terms of courage and love. I later asked Juliet to share what made her grateful about Camino:

> My reason for walking the Camino is not a primarily religious one. I am not carrying a rosary nor attempting to sit in on most of the pilgrim masses along the way. I don't consider myself

particularly religious in general. I prefer to allow my spirituality to become further defined as I learn more about the world.

Just because I don't call it heaven doesn't mean I don't take time to talk to the sky. I've found myself sending many "thank you's" and a "please" now and then upwards as we walk. When taking a journey like this, I think it's important to remember to go ahead and be grateful, send those appreciative thoughts out, even if you don't have a name yet for what or who they're meant for.

On that note, I am grateful for many things, including the following:

- Likable travel companions
- Working showers
- Spanish bread and wine
- The breeze on hot days
- My legs (and back and hips and neck)
- My language skills
- Advil
- Free potable water
- An excellent view (most of the time)
- The opportunity to walk 500 miles across Spain with beloved companions and ample time to reflect on all the things back home that I'm happy to have as well

Buen Camino,

Juliet

HOLDING OUR PLACE FOR THE
BERICANOS DEL ALBURGUE

Chapter 11

SELF-AWARENESS

Promise me you'll always remember: You're braver than you believe, and stronger than you seem, and smarter than you think.

~ Christopher Robin to Winnie the Pooh
A. A. Milne

On my first day of walking alone, I was wondering what the rest of my journey would feel like, at least until I caught up with Juliet five days later in Leon. While I wasn't afraid and was certainly capable of walking alone, it was not what I had intended. I missed Rick back home. I missed Caroline, my Camino wife, and wasn't sure how many times I could keep reinventing my Camino family. Inside I was wailing.

When I arrived by myself to the Espiritu Santos Albergue in Carrion de los Condes, the nuns of St. Vincent de Paul handed me a small medal at check-in. In tiny letters around the edge and encircling Mary were inscribed the words, "Oh Maria sin pecado consebida rogad pro nos que recurrimos a Vos." Translated, "O Mary, sinless conceived, pray for us who turn to you." Since Mary was my regular companion and confessor, I immediately put my medal on a string around my neck and hoped it would work wonders after a draining day of feeling sorry for myself.

The Espirtu Santos albergue was large, airy, and segregated by sex. I was assigned to one of four clean and basic rooms for women laid out with 15 single beds, which reminded me of pictures of WWII hospital wards. I was surprised to see one of our Swedish friends unloading her pack at the base of one of the beds. We greeted each other warmly and made plans to share dinner after mass.

Many of the services I attended along Camino moved me, but few more than the traditional Pilgrim's Mass in the 12th-century Iglesia de Santa Maria del Camino. After nearly 18 days of walking, I was at my lowest point in the journey and only halfway to my destination. I was in need of spiritual as well as emotional sustenance.

Three Augustinian nuns strummed a simple tune on the guitar. They sang in Spanish and then in English and passed around a basket filled with paper stars that they said would remind us that they were praying for us. Following this special service, the priest invited the 50 pilgrims in attendance to the front of the church for a collective blessing. Many nationalities were represented, mostly Europeans, but also Scandinavians, South Koreans, Australians, and Americans.

Before I had left the States, I asked my mom, Rose Marie, to lend me one of my grandmother's rosaries. My maternal grandmother, Marie Byrne, was a devout Catholic who would have loved the purpose behind Camino. She didn't have money to travel, certainly not to faraway places like Spain. The priest here in Carrion blessed my grandmother's humble glass rosary.

All along Camino, I would take Grandmother's rosary out when I visited modest stone churches and grand cathedrals alike, so that she, too, could have a look around.

Each time I lit a candle in the churches along The Way, I thought about the generations of strong women in my family line. It was reassuring to think that I had passed along these same genes to Juliet. While I didn't know exactly where she was, I knew that Juliet too would learn valuable lessons about life and herself on Camino. I hoped that she wasn't too young to have a conversation with herself about taking responsibility for her own happiness.

I had a good night's sleep in Carrion, and a good thing too. Typically, villages sprinkled along Camino offer a place to rest along the way. But not on the day ahead. That day's walk was a long and lonely 17-

kilometer stretch of the Meseta without shade or services.

A steady stream of pilgrims spilled out of the Espiritu Santos Albergue and other albergues at 6 a.m. in an effort to beat the forecast of nearly 100-degree heat. Warned ahead of time, I had plenty of water and food. My pack included dried apricots and hazelnuts, along with a tomato, green pepper, and half of a chorizo sausage.

I walked for several kilometers with a brother and sister traveling with an Irish college group. They set a blazingly fast pace and shared funny stories that made the walk more bearable. When they heard about my Irish lineage as a Byrne, they regaled me with the history of Clan O'Byrne and tales of its one-time leader, Fiach McHugh O'Byrne. The family's motto was, "I have fought and I have conquered." It was reassuring to hear this on a day like that one as I fought to keep my tearfulness at bay.

Meanwhile, Juliet was pressing ahead at her own fast pace. I would learn later that she had walked the 19 kilometers to Carrion as I had the day before but then tacked on this additional 17 kilometers that same afternoon. Most peregrinos avoided this demanding portion of the path in the merciless afternoon heat.

On this stretch, Juliet met two school administrators from the U.S. and began a conversation that would lead to her next step. The superintendent of a small rural school in the Aleutian Islands told Juliet that they needed teachers like her in Alaska. When she explained that she was not trained as a teacher, he replied that they were looking for individuals with her sense of adventure and exuberance. If she were interested, he could help her obtain her teaching credentials in Alaska. They exchanged email contacts and parted enthusiastically.

For my part, I was at the midway point of Camino and in the heart of Knights Templar country. I was wondering if the second half of my journey would be as rewarding as the first half when I arrived at the Jacques de Molay albergue in Terradillos de los Templarios. This old, family-run albergue was named after the last Grand Master of the Knights Templar Order who was burned at the stake in 1314. Unhappy history aside, the albergue was a friendly and lively stopping place for pilgrims. I was hoping to find some nice companionship for my evening meal.

You can imagine how delighted I was to find Caroline sitting on the grass lawn rubbing her feet. All of that praying had worked, and I was beyond relieved to be reunited with my good friend and traveling companion.

That evening, Caroline, who is neither Catholic nor deeply religious, joined me for an unusual mass with an English-speaking priest named Father Jerrod. After more than a dozen masses, I only now realized that all of them had been spoken in Spanish.

And I really don't speak Spanish. Was I kidding my-self as I followed along, even during the sermons?

A dozen pilgrims sat on wooden benches and shared where they were from. A young Italian priest with blistered feet celebrated mass alongside Father Jerrod. From the way he limped around the altar, this priest was clearly on Camino as well. When Father Jerrod asked us to share why we were each walking Camino, I struggled again with this question of why. Of course "why" is always the toughest question to answer. Perhaps it is the most important one as well. I shared that I was walking with my daughter but didn't know how to sum up what I was searching for myself.

The hot and hazy Meseta looked endless as we walked out of Terradillos through the market town of Sahagun and into Bercianos. The next few days were filled with sweat and quiet contemplation, eve-nings with sunsets and swallows.

The next stop was Leon where I had made ar-rangements to meet with Juliet outside the cathedral. Leon is another of the larger cities on the Camino Francés, its grand square in the shadow of a 13th-century Gothic gem of a cathedral. According to the audio tour, it boasted as much stained glass as Chartres Cathedral in France.

Despite the promise of Leon and a city filled with Spanish culture and history, my life had been scrubbed down to such simple needs that the traffic and bustle of a metropolis left me feeling agitated. Walking into a city was a much more confusing experience than ambling through quiet rural villages where the yellow arrows are easy to see and getting lost meant you were still only one street away.

I was sitting on a park bench in the cathedral's grand plaza when Juliet arrived. She had had a good five days. Gregarious and outgoing, Juliet had no trouble meeting people, striking up animated conversations in several languages.

Leon was another city that served as a gathering place for pilgrims, offering a rest stop with much to see. Juliet was excited to find familiar faces and catch the music festival that night. Me? I was ready to begin walking the next morning, even though the cities and towns across the Meseta were still in the midst of a brutal heat wave. For the last few days, the temperature had reached 104 degrees and didn't begin to cool down until after 8 p.m. It was easy to see why the Spanish take their siestas in the midafternoon. Shops close and everyone disappears. Only after 7 p.m. do people reemerge and fill the streets with laughter.

Juliet and I enjoyed our reunion and our walk out of Leon together, back to farm fields, a gravel track, and cork trees. Storks were everywhere. With their white bodies and long red legs, we could almost picture baby bundles clasped in their beaks. Only on the Meseta did we see storks and their enormous nests perched on high points like bell towers. Their nests are so big that other birds build their nests in them. The juveniles were almost full grown, and we watched them practice their shaky takeoffs and landings.

The Meseta is also big-time medieval country. We crossed a long and famous medieval bridge in Hospital de Órbigo that spans a large grassy field where knights had jousted in the 13th century. So much ancient history was around me that I wished I knew more about the Middle Ages and Crusades. While much of the history was lost on me, I saw the splayed red cross, the symbol of the Knights Templar, all around me.

Just beyond Hospital de Órbigo and past fields of garlic and hops, which are trained to grow vertically like pyres of pole beans, we found one of our nicest albergues. The inner courtyard where we washed and dried our clothes was filled with geraniums and hydrangeas. Juliet and I were traveling with Caroline, another Dutch woman from Delft, and two women from Singapore. These three had started walking in May in Lourdes, France, and became new friends for the rest of the walk into Santiago.

That night, 13 of us, including the Belgian owners of the albergue, enjoyed dinner in the courtyard. Our hosts served leek soup and quiche and told us about their lives in Belgium. The owner and her husband, a policeman, recently had purchased the albergue in Villares de Órbigo. Money was tight and their own quarters were in need of constant repair, but they set a lovely table and welcomed us warm-heartedly. Camino gives you a chance to meet people and hear their stories, seeing how they live and what they plant in their gardens as you contemplate the slower tempo of life in the countryside.

Just beyond the Meseta, we could see the mountains that bordered the state of Galicia in the distance. As we set out through the fields to Astorga, an ancient crossroads that dates back to Roman times, we came across David with his donativo stand. He lived in the middle of a large field, and his stand offered pilgrims hard-boiled eggs, freshly squeezed orange juice, and a surprisingly large variety of fruits, olives, and nuts. Some pilgrims choose to spend the night in David's lean-to under the Spanish stars.

Our first sight of Astorga was from a high point where an old man played the guitar. We rested for a while and he serenaded us for small change. He asked Juliet in Spanish where everyone was from and if we had anything to represent our home countries. Juliet gave him a U.S. dollar. As we walked down the hill, he sang "The American girl gave me a dollar" to some recognizable tune, I'm not sure which one.

Several pleasant days had passed, but Juliet became restless to walk at her own pace again. Caroline and I said good-bye to her in the shadow of Astorga's impressive church. We were all headed west toward the mountains of Galicia, each of us at her own pace and with our own questions to answer.

PILGRIM STATUE AT THE ALTO SAN ROQUE

Chapter 12

ENCOURAGEMENT

When I look out at the people and they look at me and they're smiling, then I know that I'm loved. That is the time when I have no worries, no problems.

~ Etta James

Everywhere we went, we were encouraged. Everywhere we went, we heard the words, "Buen Camino, Buen Camino."

Literally translated, Buen Camino means "good road." For us peregrinos, though, the phrase meant so much more. It was how we said hello and goodbye. Sometimes it meant "I'm gaining on you and passing on the left"; other times it meant "I feel your pain." But universally, these two words of encouragement meant "we're all in this together."

For a thousand years, locals along the route have been in the business—financially and spiritually—of servicing pilgrims: lodging to meet the need of every pocketbook; cafés, sometimes makeshift ones at the top of a hill; local tiendas for provisioning; and pilgrim's masses offered to those who practice and those who do not. You have no idea of how much you appreciate the sight of a chair after several hours of walking. Just a chair!

I came to appreciate messages of encouragement in unexpected places, like the word "forgive" spelled out in stones on the path, or the graffiti with words of support painted on the side of a building. Messages came in all languages. Some were elaborate poems inscribed in city tunnels; others were simple messages of a Buen Camino found along rural byways. Often we would see a hiking boot filled with flowers. I wondered if the pilgrim hopped away or just ditched the other boot.

One day we came across a fallen tree with the inscription, "Be with the one who makes you happy." Except that the word "with" was crossed out, giving you two ways to think about the message. Another message, on the side of an oversized green trash can, reminded us, "Don't forget who you are." It became part of the journey to look for the messages, reflecting on their meaning and appreciating the more memorable or provocative graffiti.

We were also surrounded by people available to help. Whether they were locals in the villages who were happy to point us in the right direction or hospitaleros who provided lodging, food, and hugs, we never lacked for a network of support.

A favorite moment came as we walked into the outskirts of Belorado where we were welcomed by three members of the Swiss confraternity. Caroline and I had stopped to rest in front of the Santa Maria y San Pedro, an old church with four enormous storks' nests perched on the upper reaches of its bell tower. The church backed up to a hillside with an overgrown path leading to an overlook where we had our own bird's-eye view of the red roofs of town below and the nests, balanced improbably, just out of arms' reach.

Members of the Swiss team of hospitaleros were rotating through a three-week volunteer assignment. Their job was to provide a warm welcome and see to every conceivable need of the pilgrims. Their days were long. They were often the first to rise in the morning to prepare breakfast, shooing peregrinos out the door by 8 a.m. so they could ready rooms for the next batch of weary walkers. The team members were also the last to bed at night, some providing an evening meal after which they would wash up, solve a variety of daily dilemmas and, I assume, fall finally into their own humble accommodations at the end of a long day.

Our Swiss hosts offered tea, chocolate, and a diagnosis of aches and pains. The sign on the door said "Dolor de pies, dolores y molestias? El diagnóstico de cinco euro donativo." In English, "Sore feet, aches and pains? Diagnosis for a 5 euro donation."

Since I had developed sciatica and was rolling my left foot on my tennis ball, I thought the five euros would be well worth it. And boy, it was! An 81-year-old Swiss reflexologist named Arturo cracked our backs, found our pressure points, and even diagnosed our emotional ailments. Since Caroline spoke German, she understood Arturo well when he said that her problem point led straight to the gallbladder, where she was storing too much bile. Arturo asked Caroline why she was so angry and advised that her anger was causing her pain. This realization—and what she would later tell me was a confirmation of what she already knew—led to tears. All of our emotions were close to the surface.

One of the most encouraging aspects of Camino was the ethic of sharing, no matter how little you had to begin with or how much you might need of what you were giving away. We shared everything from accommodations and med kits to stories and life lessons. I shared my love of Three Dog Night with Caroline, and she danced her way up a few hills singing "Never Been to Spain." Juliet and I shared a lot of laughs with two good-humored young Danes who would smoke cigarettes and drink beer at second breakfast, sprinting ahead and then crashing along the trail for an afternoon nap. We shared moleskin, Compeed, and every home remedy to take good care of our feet.

I was happy to share my carefully selected supplies since my feet were still in good shape. I hoped that my good fortune would continue and that I would be as generous even if my luck changed. My feet were callused in all the right places but not rubbed raw from hours of walking like so many others.

I was, however, still plagued with a persistent bout of sciatica. My tennis ball, a gift from Pepe, got lost somewhere along the way and I learned to walk through the pain, like everyone else. Camino attracts a fair share of those of us walking boldly into our second half century, so nearly everyone was dealing with one or another body ache in their feet, knees, and backs.

Camino has a way of uniting people around a common purpose, and the concept of sharing—advice, supplies, and support—is central to this walk. Very different from more solitary hikes on the Appalachian or Pacific Crest Trails, this walk has everything to do with the people you meet and the conversations you have as you walk. If you are looking for a less social walk, Camino is not your best bet.

Mostly we shared respect. Respect for each other, for the land, and for our little place in Camino history. We also shared respect for the code of the Camino. I'm not sure that the "code" is written down anywhere, but the observance of common courtesies could deeply affect our daily quality of life. We lived in close quarters, sharing bedrooms and bathrooms. As limited as our belongings were, keeping them neat and tidy was important. Staying quiet while others tried to rest was also appreciated. Most peregrinos were discreet and, while modesty suffered a bit, we were rewarded with a new and ever-changing mix of like-minded individuals, all moving in the same direction along the same path.

No matter our nationality, we shared equally in basic needs, not just for food, lodging, and rest, but for peace and companionship. Camino has a way of reminding us that we get what we give.

After 25 days of walking, we were approaching the Cruz de Ferros, the highest point on Camino. But first we would make a stop in the village of Rabanal, staying at an albergue run by the English-based Confraternity of St. James. Here I enjoyed the 5 p.m. ritual of high tea served on a breezy terrace followed by 7 p.m. vespers in the simple, rough-hewn church of Santa Maria next door. When would be the next time I got the chance to listen to Gregorian chanting by Benedictine monks?

Since it was July 3rd and two of the three volunteers in our English albergue were from Idaho, we celebrated the honor of being Americans by singing a round of "America the Beautiful" at 6:15 a.m. the next morning. As much as I love to travel, I felt so privileged to be an American. At one point during the walk that day, I heard a strain of "Me and Bobby

McGee," which made me cry and pine for home. I thought, "How lucky am I?"

CAFÉ CON LECHE WITH ARROW

Chapter 13

FORGIVENESS

We are punished by our sins, not for them.

~ Elbert Hubbard

Mothers and daughters have a special place in heaven, although I'm not sure that they are always seated right next to each other. There is nothing wrong with a healthy distance. It's not easy to be a mother or a daughter, untangling the emotions that come with the territory.

I thought a lot about being a mom on Camino. How could I not? At times, I was in full mom-mode, giving advice to help Juliet grow up to be healthy, productive, well-adjusted, and respectful. I said that she should find her own way, but I was pretty inclined to give her a map. I wanted her to be happy and independent, but I sometimes didn't know how to get my boot off her neck so Juliet could get on with being who she wanted to be.

At the same time that I was so sure I had most of the answers, Camino offered an opportunity for me to come face-to-face with my own shortcomings. Reflecting on my own imperfections helped me to remember that I was still a work in progress.

For example, I analyzed my demanding nature, which often led to a critical outlook on what I characterize as mediocrity. If you look for mediocrity, you will find it all around. You can imagine how exhausting it was to always be dissatisfied with the work of others. How often had I remade the beds and rewritten the memo? I could hear myself grumble, "Why not just do the job right the first time?"

I was equally demanding in my battle against injustice and inconsideration, ready to ensure that others improved their game, whether they agreed with me or not.

As a former debater, it is part of my DNA to be sure that everyone understands my point. I used to refer to it as "honest communications." Too often, though, my honest communications were delivered to loved ones with a rhetorical bludgeon. I would bang a point home until I could see the whites of their eyes. The process left everyone abundantly clear about what I was saying but occasionally on the floor in a puddle.

But perhaps the imperfection I hated and feared the most in me was my tendency toward resentment. This feeling of being slighted or unappreciated lived just below the surface for me. I would try so hard to let little grievances go until I reached a tipping point—usually when I was tired—when all that backed-up frustration spewed out. I was a prisoner to my own unrealistic expectations and perceived slights.

So I had plenty of work to do on me. When we reached the highest point of Camino at 5,000 feet, the Cruz de Ferro, I had plenty for which to seek forgiveness.

The Cruz de Ferro or Iron Cross is not grand or ornate but has become an enduring symbol of Camino. The tradition is to leave behind a stone that signifies what's negative in your world and should be left behind. Before Juliet and I left on Camino, Rick gave us each a piece of coal he had found washed up on the beaches of Assateague Island.

Since coal turns into diamonds under pressure, Rick's sentiment was a lovely metaphor for a tough journey that would polish and make us sparkle like diamonds. Juliet and I reached the Cruz a day apart, but we both left our pieces of coal at its base. I actually tied mine to the base of the cross, hoping that it wouldn't get nudged aside as quickly by pilgrims who followed.

The Cruz is an emotional moment for many pilgrims. Many leave their tears there. For me, I was not overcome by my emotions at the Cruz, perhaps because I had already done my share of praying and pleading for forgiveness, mostly in the churches throughout the journey. I remember giving a hug to a woman from California who was overwrought with the grief of losing her father. I was later told by other pilgrims that she mentioned my name and how much the hug helped her get past a moment of suffering.

After spending two hours thinking, praying, and regarding the stones and tokens left behind at the Cruz, Caroline and I set out through the mountains to Acebo. The route was steep and full of scree, but we were paid off in terms of exceptional views into deep valleys as well as the purple heather that lined our path. I took my only fall on the rocky path when my feet slipped out from underneath me. Luckily my pack took the brunt of the fall.

At our parochial albergue in Acebo, we were asked to leave our packs in the entryway and take only what we needed upstairs to our bunks. We encountered new faces and enjoyed a simple communal dinner of salad, lentil soup, and chocolate rice pudding. A Danish brother and sister brought out their ukulele after dinner, and we sang American favorites in honor of Independence Day. After dinner, Mother Nature treated us to a fine sunset with a rough-hewn wooden cross in the foreground and the impressive Asturia mountain range in the distance.

As the days wore on, so did I. It didn't matter that we were walking through picturesque vineyards that produce the regional Bierzo wines. The mind-bending sunshine and rocky slopes of this rural mountain region left me frustrated and near heat-stroke. Like a six-year-old, I wanted to sit down in the middle of the path and cry. One day, I kept seeing signs for Cacabelos, our stopping point for the night—but no town. "Where is the fucking town?" I bawled.

Similar to making a transfer of flights in an airline terminal, I was disembarking on one flight and getting onto another for the final leg of my Camino journey. I was experiencing a mix of emotions around getting ready to be done. I was feeling insecure, bitchy, and exhausted. These emotions kept bubbling up, catching me by surprise.

The next day, once again, I said a tearful good-bye to Caroline and set out for O Cebreiro where I would meet Juliet. O Cebreiro is the gateway to Galicia, and Juliet and I had promised each other that we would walk through Galicia and into Santiago together.

O Cebreiro is a small village at the top of a monumental crest and an important pilgrim mecca on The Way. The Pilgrim's Mass and blessing at 7 p.m. was particularly moving in its simple 9th-century church with its statue of the Santa Maria la Real displayed for pilgrims and tourists to see. I picked up the Pilgrim's Prayer printed on postcards just inside the door and was happy to leave a one-euro donation, as suggested.

I met Juliet outside of the church. She had ridden into O Cebreiro on Luna, a feisty five-year-old horse. She spoke Spanish to Luna, who liked to be in front and occasionally took off no matter what language she heard. It sounded to me like they were well suited for each other.

Now reunited, mother and daughter had been walking—sometimes together and sometimes apart—for 28 days, putting us about eight days from Santiago, depending upon our pace. We were happy to be walking together again, having benefited from the time spent apart. We both had stories to tell about our experiences along the same path. It was getting easier to be optimistic about our approaching success and to enjoy the views without the worries I felt in the Pyrenees or on the Meseta.

Our views were spectacular and green with deep valleys and layers upon layers of Galician mountains. We walked through forests, Galician villages stuck in time, and, as we moved into lower altitudes, past farm fields of corn and cows. It was a feast of sights, sounds, and smells. As we traveled past farm after farm, we were assaulted by the pungent mix of manure and hay. In fact, sometimes we didn't need the yellow arrow, as the cow patties pointed the way.

Beginning in Sarria, we were in the final 100-kilometer stretch to Santiago. Sarria is the starting point for many pilgrims, so the route was busy with fresh feet. Teams of Spanish schoolkids sang loudly as they walked, a few of them on bowed legs from the chafing between their thighs.

Along one forest track, we heard the plaintiff strains of a bagpipe, and then we saw the piper, in traditional Galician dress. Galicia has a strong Celtic influence; hence the bagpipes or gaita along with Celtic crosses seen along this section of The Way. Even the weather and the landscape resembled western Ireland. Typical of Galicia were the free-standing granaries or horreros, some purely for decoration, others being used for their originally intended purpose of storing grain.

Juliet and I rested in increasingly crowded cafés, chatting with old and new friends and eating egg sandwiches. We caught up with Caroline at an albergue run by a South African man named Gordon. Flags from all over the world hung in the courtyard. The eight available beds were filled with American, Dutch, Swedish, German, and Danish women. We concluded our dinner of pimientos de padron and chicken curry with a few songs and an after dinner liquor called hierbas.

As I walked, getting closer to the finish line, I thought about how Marv Levy, former head coach of the Buffalo Bills, used to motivate his players. He would ask them, "Where else would you rather be than right here right now?" I was certain that there was no place I'd rather be than where I was at that moment.

That didn't mean that I wasn't ready to be done. That didn't mean that I wasn't eager to see Rick and Danny. I had enjoyed every step of this journey despite the tears, the fatigue, and a certain degree of friction between Juliet and me. I was grateful that I was physically and emotionally strong enough to walk 500 miles even though it wasn't always easy.

PILGRIM AT THE CRUZ DE FERRO

―――――――― Chapter 14 ――――――――

REWARD

*This is, in the end, your life to live. It is time
to move on and create something new.*

Five hundred miles and 35 days from the day we
started, Juliet and I walked into Santiago. I was
overwhelmed with a mix of emotions that I couldn't
quite describe. The air was filled with street music
and singing. Pilgrims greeted each other with hugs
and congratulations. I certainly felt accomplished,
and even relieved. The old city was exciting and bus-
tling with locals, tourists, and pilgrims.

Juliet and I headed straight for the Pilgrim's Office where we handed over our credentials and received our Compostela, along with a certificate of
distance that verified 775 kilometers. Colorful and
written in Latin, I'm still not exactly sure what these

documents say. Are they proof of my closer relationship with God?

I was then struck. Now what? Well, we needed a place to stay, and I definitely needed a glass of Albarino wine. We had the rest of the afternoon to sort things out before we met up with Caroline for dinner. Here at my intended destination, I was feeling a bit lost.

Have you ever had that moment when you achieved what you set out to accomplish, yet it didn't feel like the crowning moment you expected? Had I already checked the Camino off the list and demanded of myself what was next? Did I expect to feel a more final sense of accomplishment? Where was this elusive thing called closure?

The following morning, I was still feeling unmoored. I thought that a visit to the Cathedral of Santiago for the Pilgrim's Mass might give me the sense of finality that I was missing. Since Juliet and I had walked into Santiago close to noon, I had saved this special mass for the next day. I didn't want to rush my experience at the cathedral. Since I knew the mass was held daily, I could be rested and ready for the final pilgrim's blessing.

When I arrived at 10 a.m. the next day, Polish, French, and German masses were underway in small chapels around the edge of the grand cathedral. I found a smattering of Irish and English pilgrims sitting on folding chairs in a corner alcove waiting for the English-speaking service to begin. I joined them in quiet contemplation.

The main event was the Pilgrim's Mass held at noon. This mass was celebrated by priests from around the world, each performing sections of the mass in his native language. Every pew was filled, and more pilgrims crowded the aisles and perched on stone ledges. Even Juliet attended to witness the swinging of the giant incense burner or Botafumeiro. It swung high over our heads, the heavy ropes worked by six men in cranberry-colored velvet robes. The Botafumeiro is a big crowd pleaser, although its beginnings lie in fumigating stinky pilgrims.

After mass, Juliet and I hiked to the bus station to catch a bus to the coast. Finisterre, which translates into Land's End, is a stop for pilgrims who want to continue on after Santiago. Finisterre had its origins in an ancient pagan belief that the sun died every day at Land's End, only to be reborn again the next day. The ritual of visiting Finisterre includes burning something you no longer want, usually an article of clothing or paper. Juliet and I wrote out the notes we would burn during our own ceremony on the rocks overlooking the Atlantic. Unfortunately, the gusty winds kept blowing out our lighter, so we didn't burn anything but our fingertips.

Only when we watched the sun set at the Finisterre lighthouse was I finally able to say "the end." Once thought to be the westernmost point of Europe, Finisterre did indeed feel like the land's end. We saw the coastline and lighthouse from the best vantage possible—a boat. And my compliments to whoever selected the music—Celtic chords provided an atmospheric backdrop until we got to the furthest-most point when they played Led Zeppelin's "Stairway to Heaven." Ole!

FINISTERRE

By David Whyte from *Pilgrim*
Reprinted with permission

The road in the end taking the path the sun had taken,
into the western sea, and the moon rising behind you
as you stood where ground turned to ocean: no way
to your future now but the way your shadow could take,
walking before you across water, going where shadows go,
no way to make sense of a world that wouldn't let you pass
except to call an end to the way you had come,
to take out each frayed letter you had brought
and light their illumined corners; and to read
them as they drifted on the late western light;
to empty your bags; to sort this and to leave that;
to promise what you needed to promise all along,
and to abandon the shoes that brought you here
right at the water's edge, not because you had given up
but because now, you would find a different way to tread,
and because, through it all, part of you would still walk on,
no matter how, over the waves.

I certainly saw my daughter in a new light during this adventure. Not without a few scrapes along the way, I'm happy to say we were able to firmly establish a new kind of relationship, still mother-daughter but more on an adult level. I witnessed Juliet's resilience and strength, carrying a 30-pound pack for 500 miles, her sheer and utter fearlessness, her compassion toward others, and her effervescence for life. I know she learned a few new things about me too.

Sometimes the hardest journeys offer the greatest rewards. I love the concept of reaching deep and pressing through the difficult bits to get to the other side. Because you know what you find there? The confidence to know that you can do anything.

As a result of the million steps that Juliet and I took from St. Jean Pied-de-Port to Santiago de Compostela, Juliet landed that job teaching school in the Aleutian Islands of Alaska. When Juliet returned home, she contacted Michael and Hillary whom she had met on her long walk across the hot stretch of the Meseta. Immediately, they set up a Skype interview with the Sand Point School Board and, that same evening, offered Juliet a position teaching Spanish in Alaska. It was a Tuesday, and she had to be there the following Monday, so Juliet had to act fast.

As for me, I stayed in touch with a few close Camino friends, including Caroline and Chuck. A veteran walker, Chuck was arranging a trek to the Annapurna Circuit in Nepal and offered me the opportunity to walk in the Himalayas the following October. When I asked Rick what he thought, he encouraged me to go.

And so I set off on a new adventure to Nepal. But I will save that story for another day.

As I closed this chapter, I took a next inspired step in the direction I wanted to go. It turned out to be another long walk. I took that walk even though I wasn't sure exactly where it would lead. After all, you can't see too far down the road; you can only see the next step.

Whatever next step you take, don't wait to begin. Buen Camino!

JULIET AND TRACY
AT THE SANTIAGO STONE MARKER

EPILOGUE

The beginning is always today.

~ Mary Shelley

As I finish writing this book, it's been more than two years since Juliet and I walked Camino. Juliet spent a year teaching Spanish, music, and art to her students in Sand Point, Alaska, a remote corner of the world, even if it is still the United States. Now back in Pennsylvania, she recently completed her certification to teach English as a foreign language and is awaiting an overseas assignment, her sights set on a Spanish-speaking country. We can't wait to see where she will go next. One thing is for certain: her big sense of adventure is alive and well, and she is hungrier than ever to experience new cultures and faraway places.

My adventure continues too. Rick and I decided to change our setting and moved out of the neighborhood and onto a few acres of land with nature all around us. We're still close to civilization, but it feels like we are a million miles away. I took a new job consulting with small businesses and nonprofits. It gives me more time and flexibility to balance my priorities around family, work, and travel. I've continued walking and have completed long-distance walks on several continents. None of them have been like Camino, but that's okay. None have had the spiritual impact I experienced on the Way of St. James, but each offered a chance to slow down and immerse myself in a new landscape, one I wouldn't be able to appreciate from the window of a car or train.

Caroline is still a big presence in my life, even from her home in Amsterdam. We have visited together once and plan to do so again. Thank goodness for What's App and the free calls we can make to keep caught up on each other's lives. She's getting ready to make a move too, needing a change of scenery to satisfy her post-Camino restlessness.

I still ask myself today, what did I learn on Camino?

I learned that Camino is a powerful metaphor to remind us about life's timeless truths. Understanding these truths keeps us connected to each other and helps us discern what brings happiness to our lives. And, as far as we know, we only get one go-round in life, so it's important to have a little faith—and remember, a little is all it takes—to take the next step in the direction we want to go.

I've come to understand that the deepest journey of Camino doesn't begin until the pilgrim arrives back home. While I keep moving in the direction I want to go, some days are better than others. It's easy to forget the promises I made to myself on Camino. Life's journey is not without friction and doubt. I find that hanging onto the mindfulness of Camino is one of the biggest challenges for me. My battle to forgive myself, at the heart of much of my own personal strife, was not embedded in a lump of coal and left behind at the Cruz de Ferro.

Just as Camino offered me the great gift of time and space to reflect on life's questions, I realize now not all the answers can be found in a 35-day window. They linger and persist. In fact, the questions change over time even if you had the right questions in the first place.

It turns out that *my* Camino was the road leading me back to my faith. Going to mass regularly and praying have become a lasting part of my routine. I'm still praying for forgiveness and I'm still not quite sure exactly why. My connection to the Virgin Mary is still present, and I keep my grandmother's rosary close by. As I think about how I felt about all those sermons I listened to in Spanish—not understanding the words but being touched by their meaning—I believe that Camino sparked my desire to comprehend and *apprehend* my faith. Clearly I was hungry for that kind of sustenance.

In addition to my deepened relationship with Juliet, my rekindled relationship with God has been one of the greatest gifts Camino gave to me. Camino offered an opportunity to strip away the distractions of everyday life so that I could have a deeper, more spiritual conversation with myself and my faith.

And so The Way continues.

Santiago was just a beginning!

ABOUT THE AUTHOR

While this is Tracy Pawelski's first book, she is no stranger to the power of words. Professionally, Tracy combines corporate communications experience with a background in politics and public policy. Her work has taken her from the halls of the U.S. Congress and the boardrooms of Corporate America to grocery store aisles around the world as she looked for compelling stories and hot button issues.

As the former vice president of communications for a global retail grocer, Tracy oversaw strategies for public relations, crisis communications, and community engagement. She managed a charitable foundation committed to the fight against hunger and improving the quality of life for children. Before returning to her roots in Pennsylvania, Tracy worked on national issues in the Office of National Drug Control Policy and U.S. House of Representatives, Washington, D.C.

Tracy is an adventure traveler, preferring destinations out of the mainstream and activities that make your heart thump. She has published travel articles on these adventures, including a story about the fear that she faced on the side of a mountain while skiing in British Columbia's back country.

In addition to walking 500 miles on El Camino de Santiago, Tracy recently trekked the Annapurna Circuit in Nepal and the West Highland Way in Scotland. Tracy and her husband, Rick, teach skiing in the winter at a local mountain where Tracy's father was a founding ski patroller.

Tracy and Rick live in Central Pennsylvania where they enjoy hiking on the nearby Appalachian Trail, riding a tandem bicycle, and date-night yoga. Daughter, Juliet, teaches English in San Jose, Costa Rica, where she can put her fluent Spanish-speaking skills to good use. Son Danny lives and works in Colorado, where he can ski the trees as often as possible.

Tracy speaks to groups about her pilgrimage on El Camino in addition to travel and trekking, getting inspired, leadership in action, and the challenges faced by professional women. She's waiting to hear from you!

WWW.TRACYPAWELSKI.COM